I, ISAAC, *take* THEE, REBEKAH

BY RAVI ZACHARIAS

THOMAS NELSON
Since 1798

NASHVILLE   DALLAS   MEXICO CITY   RIO DE JANEIRO   BEIJING

Published in Nashville, Tennessee, by Thomas Nelson. Thomas Nelson is a registered trademark of Thomas Nelson, Inc.

Thomas Nelson, Inc. titles may be purchased in bulk for educational, business, fundraising, or sales promotional use. For information, please e-mail SpecialMarkets@ThomasNelson.com.

All Scripture quotations, unless otherwise indicated, are taken from The Holy Bible, New International Version (NIV), © 1973, 1978, 1984 by International Bible Society. Used by permission of Zondervan Publishing House.

Other Scripture references are from the following sources:

The New King James Version (NKJV®), © 1979, 1980, 1982, Thomas Nelson, Inc., Publishers.

The King James Version of the Bible (KJV).

Library of Congress Cataloging-in-Publication Data

Zacharias, Ravi K.
   I, Isaac, take thee, Rebekah / by Ravi Zacharias.
   p. cm.
   ISBN 978-0-8499-0822-4
   1. Marriage—Religious aspects—Christianity. 2. Marriage—Biblical teaching.
3. Isaac (Biblical patriarch) 4. Rebekah (Biblical matriarch) 5. Bible. O.T. Genesis—Criticism, interpretation, etc. I. Title.
BV835.Z33 2004
248.4—dc22   2003022171

Printed in the United States of America

08 09 10 11 12 QW 9 8 7 6 5

TO JEAN AND LINDSAY REYNOLDS

who have just celebrated their sixtieth anniversary.

A Testimony to God, A Tribute to each other, An Example to us.

With my love and gratitude.

Contents

ACKNOWLEDGMENTS

In every effort undertaken there are those behind the scenes who work very hard to bring a message to print. I should begin by thanking Dr. James Dobson of Focus on the Family for making the spoken version of this message well-recognized and appreciated all over the world. I must also thank my assistant Nancy Bevers for her encouragement over many years to write these thoughts down. Once I finished the manuscript the workload was carried by my wife, Margie, as she pored over every page. She, of course has edited all my books but of them all, this one made me the most nervous because she was the "proofreader" not only for the content, but for evaluating its very application in my own life. That was a bit nerve-wracking to me, to say the least. But as always, she was gracious in her critique and contribution. In that sense, the very theme of this book has been lived out by her. How can one gainsay that? My thanks also to Danielle DuRant, my research assistant, for finding some resource help for me and for her contribution in readying the manuscript for publication.

I would be remiss if I did not say a heartfelt word of thanks to our children—Sarah, Naomi and Nathan. They have been understanding, patient and forgiving over the years. With a lifestyle that has involved so much travel over three decades, they could have easily become embittered or cynical. But their love has remained strong and constantly affirming. They are three rays of sunshine when the road of life can sometimes get dark. They make me feel better than I am and that is purely an act of grace. I owe them a debt I cannot repay.

Finally, my sincere thanks to David Moberg, Allen Arnold, and Thomas Nelson, Inc. for the trust they had in assigning this book to me. I am grateful.

RAVI ZACHARIAS
Atlanta, Georgia

INTRODUCTION

S ome subjects you address because they rise to the top of your thinking and you sense a deep compulsion in your heart about them. No matter what other issues you consider, that one deep, pressing theme makes its way into your conversations or your preaching. Such a theme is timeless, and to fail to deal with it is to fail yourself and others. But sometimes, with the passing of time, the urgency lessens and you move on to other ideas that occupy your thoughts. The momentous subject that once held you captive no longer elicits the same fervor and passion that once overwhelmed you.

The subject of love, romance, and marriage, as I originally

addressed it in a sermon of the same title as this book captured my thinking and energy. It may have been because I, too, was making decisions that would shape my future and so felt drawn to the ramifications of these life-defining determinations. It may have also been that for the first time I was keenly aware of the direction our culture was headed and of the seeds that were being sown in society for the destruction of the home.

As the years went by, I found myself thrown constantly into a different arena, where I was called upon to defend the gospel in hostile settings. My mind was inexorably drawn to "weightier" matters of philosophical debate about truth and belief in God. That still remains my primary locus of speaking.

Yet I have sensed that sooner or later, when outward resistance to the gospel has been dismantled, some very troubling questions lie beneath the surface for the person challenging biblical truth. Young people in particular run into romance and love with an irresistible urge and then begin to wonder if love ever was, indeed, all it was made out to be.

According to a recent study by a major university, the average college student pursues "sex without strings and marriage without rings."[1] Physical intimacy is commonplace, considered just another way to have fun. And many young people aren't interested in marital commitment. They say that living together is better than the risks of marriage and the hoops they will have to go through to get out of it, the certainty of which is only a matter of time. Yet in the midst of this scene, the average person continues to hope and long that it will be otherwise.

Love is still what people long for. It is still the theme of dreams. Why else do we hear so many songs about love when all around we see shattered dreams and wrecked homes? Why is there such hype about sex when, for many, no one person seems to be able to hold our attraction? Why do we still dream and yearn and hope when those yearnings seem unrequited? Suddenly, the issues that were deemed weightier become less pressing than the matters that directly reflect life and how to live it.

For the last forty years, the home has been under steady attack from various groups, and concepts that were once cherished are now minimized and even mocked. Yet our hunger for love and a lifelong partnership still remains.

In fact, as I write this, I have just returned from the sixtieth anniversary celebration of my wife's parents' marriage. Sixty years! What a tribute to them! What an example they are to us who follow after them! Everyone to whom I have mentioned this event has responded in the same way: "You don't hear of that very often anymore." A sad commentary, I should say. Such enduring commitment is rare and almost vanishing. One card they received read, "The only thing more romantic than newly weds . . . is oldly weds." Who can deny such a tribute? Our hearts yearn for a love that lasts and is faithful.

To deal with such a hunger for fulfilled love, I turn to the subject once again. Now, almost as looking through a rearview mirror, I am well aware that objects are nearer than they appear and should be handled with care. These most fundamental truths have resurfaced to me with a deepening conviction that they are never limited to a time or a generation or even to a society. These are timeless truths that every generation must come to terms with. I have thought deeply again on these matters as requests that I write about this subject have poured in from all over the world.

I, Isaac, Take Thee, Rebekah is my response to that conviction and call. After all, it may not be an overstatement to say that a person makes heaven or hell on earth depending on the one he or she marries. Any married person will agree, with a groan or a smile. Marriage is an extraordinary relationship. It is a commitment from which you dare not take a vacation. It demands nurture and care, and like a tender shoot, the better the care, the better the blossom. But to be sure, it is hard work.

Different cultures view marriage differently. If we are not careful, we can begin to believe that marriage is society's idea within the framework of each culture and, therefore, we may deal with it as we will. Nothing could be further from the truth. Marriage was God's idea, and He alone has the right to define how it was meant to be. Within these pages I have made an effort to present God's intention for marriage as given to us in His Word. Sooner or later we all come to the realization that only when we do marriage God's way do we reap the benefits. When we do marriage our way, we damage His intent and pay the price.

Join me in this journey, begun by a servant who went looking on behalf of his master for a wife for his master's son. In that journey we will come to comprehend what it really means to say, "I take you . . . to be my lawful wedded husband" or, "I take you . . . to be my lawful wedded wife." Those words of "taking" are really words of "giving." Few things are more important than that we truly understand what they mean and the true happiness they bring.

I

THE INDISPENSABLE ELEMENT IN LOVE

*Just as strength is a man's charm,
so charm is a woman's strength.*

❖

Every spring along the streets of Delhi, huge processions follow an elegantly arrayed bridegroom on a white horse as he rides, sometimes for many miles, to the home of his bride. The horse is draped in colorful velvet. The groom sits tall, with the posture of a victor coming to claim the prize for which he has worked all his life. His attire is shining, with gold-intertwined threads falling from his turban and covering his face. Musicians, many of whom desperately need music lessons, serenade him with flutes and other instruments along his journey. These musicians rent out their services for such occasions, and though they try hard, their pathetic overestimation of their musical prowess is the subject of many jokes. Thankfully the added noise of congested streets drowns out some of the painful and off-key sounds that give the term "strain" when attached to music a whole different meaning. But frankly, amid such revelry, who really cares about these secondary matters? The musicians are there merely as accessories, not as the centerpiece.

Women carrying lighted kerosene lamps walk as part of the procession, providing a light along the darker roads and a brilliant symbol of the festive occasion. Hundreds, sometimes thousands, of guests shout and dance as they follow along toward the celebration that awaits them. As the bride's home comes into view, the music reaches a crescendo and the procession comes to a halt. Awaiting their arrival are the guests of the bride, and the massive tent set up for the feast suddenly becomes a beehive of activity. At this moment, all the attention is on the bride, bedecked in her magnificent and radiantly colored sari, her face covered by a veil, her hands and arms painted with henna in beautiful patterns.

Wedding processions are a fun part of life in those teeming cities of India. As a youngster I stood on the side of the road and watched dozens of them from a distance. I must also make a confession. With the weddings as large as they are, nobody knows who comes as whose guest. Often, as we watched a wedding procession going by, my buddies and I would bring our cricket game to a halt, casually join the groom's party of followers, and arrive along with them at the bride's home, ready to enjoy a gala dinner. During wedding season we could have feasted every night and no host would have been any the wiser. In fact, it is customary for wedding invitations to read, "We invite you, your family, and friends . . ."

I have to admit that looking back on those days of youthful

exuberance, I find my immodest self-invitations quite embarrassing to confess. Oh, but what meals we enjoyed, the best of Indian cuisine, justifying our participation as celebrants at a solemn ceremony! The truth is, we could not have cared less about the solemnity of the occasion. The food is what we came for. Priests chanted and recited incantations, but that was not for us. Weddings came and went, and I never stopped to think of what it all really meant beneath the exterior trappings.

That is why the first time I ever witnessed a wedding as an invited guest has remained etched in my memory. I accompanied my parents for the marriage of a close family friend. The ceremony took place in a church. The organ rolled, the guests rose, and the bride entered the church in a magnificent white-and-gold sari. She walked toward the groom waiting at the altar, where they pledged their vows to each other. Seeing this prompted a whirlwind of emotion within me. It was then that I began to ask questions about what it meant to be "man and wife." How did they meet? When did they decide to be married? Who did the asking? What does it mean to be in love? Does anyone ever get turned down? Is marriage forever? What if it is a mistake? What happens now? Can marriage get boring? I never doubted the sense of awe and beauty in the ceremony. There was charm in the air. But I wondered if this was all a veneer or the real thing.

Certainly the Christian world-view has a unique perspective

on marriage; yet even then cultural aspects come into play—some good, some questionable, and others, however well intended, inflicting more pain than pleasure. I am convinced that marriage is at once the most powerful union and the most misunderstood relationship we can experience. Like everything of intrinsic value, its use or abuse determines delight or devastation. To understand marriage God's way is to carry a cherished dream into reality. To violate its built-in pattern is to mangle beauty and plunder one's own riches.

Let me therefore begin with a text of Scripture that carries all the essential elements of what God had in mind when He asked us to say, "I do."

A LOVELY STORY

A heart-gripping story is told in Genesis, chapter 24. From this narrative I will build my entire framework for *I, Isaac, Take Thee, Rebekah*. I truly pray that you may find your heart enthralled by the truths we uncover and your mind stirred to think of this union in God's way and not ours. If you will, this story is the lifting of the veil, showing us what goes on behind the scenes in the making of a beautiful relationship. Some of our most important decisions are made before we utter those words of commitment to someone else.

First, let me present the background to this story. The patriarch

Abraham, a symbol of a life lived by faith, is in his last days on earth. He calls to his side his senior most servant. This servant is not named, but most Bible commentators believe he is Eliezer, who was mentioned in an earlier context. Abraham gives him a mission—indeed, his greatest one to this point: "I would like you to go back to the home of my fathers and find a young woman from among my people to be my son Isaac's wife" (see Genesis 24:3–4).

That was the charge. Eliezer was in a quandary. He didn't know how to meet this kind of demand. It was an enormous responsibility to place upon anyone. Lest you and I misunderstand this, Abraham and his servant had developed a very trusting relationship that had been proven over a protracted period of time. This was not just a menial task committed to someone who worked for him.

Time being a real concern due to Abraham's failing health, Eliezer immediately prepared for his journey and began with a passionate prayer to God. This is how the Bible tells the story:

> Then the servant took ten of his master's camels and left, taking with him all kinds of good things from his master. He set out for [Mesopotamia] and made his way to the town of Nahor. He had the camels kneel down near the well outside the town; it was toward evening, the time the women go out to draw water.
>
> Then he prayed, "O LORD, God of my master Abraham, give

me success today, and show kindness to my master Abraham. See, I am standing beside this spring, and the daughters of the townspeople are coming out to draw water. May it be that when I say to a girl, 'Please let down your jar that I may have a drink,' and she says, 'Drink, and I'll water your camels too'—let her be the one you have chosen for your servant Isaac. By this I will know that you have shown kindness to my master.'"

Before he had finished praying, Rebekah came out with her jar on her shoulder. She was the daughter of Bethuel son of Milcah, who was the wife of Abraham's brother Nahor. The girl was very beautiful, a virgin; no man had ever lain with her. She went down to the spring, filled her jar and came up again.

The servant hurried to meet her and said, "Please give me a little water from your jar."

"Drink, my lord," she said, and quickly lowered the jar to her hands and gave him a drink.

After she had given him a drink, she said, "I'll draw water for your camels too, until they have finished drinking." So she quickly emptied her jar into the trough, ran back to the well to draw more water, and drew enough for all his camels. Without saying a word, the man watched her closely to learn whether or not the LORD had made his journey successful.

When the camels had finished drinking, the man took out a gold nose ring weighing a beka and two gold bracelets weighing ten shekels. Then he asked, "Whose daughter are you?

Please tell me, is there room in your father's house for us to spend the night?"

She answered him, "I am the daughter of Bethuel, the son that Milcah bore to Nahor." And she added, "We have plenty of straw and fodder, as well as room for you to spend the night."

Then the man bowed down and worshipped the LORD, saying, "Praise be to the LORD, the God of my master Abraham, who has not abandoned his kindness and faithfulness to my master. As for me, the LORD has led me on the journey to the house of my master's relatives." (Genesis 24:10–27)

IN THE BEGINNING

This is the kind of story from which movies should be made—camels, a well, a devout man, a beautiful woman coming to draw water, a suspenseful encounter. A fleece is laid and, lo and behold, the sign follows. Ah, but that is only the veil. Let us remove the veil and catch a real glimpse of what is underneath.

The reason everyone enjoys a story like this is that each of us has a heart that beats for love and romance. When I first started preaching as a teenager, I remember quoting some humorous poetry that I can still recite from memory:

Love is like an onion—
You taste it with delight,

But when it's gone you wonder
Whatever made you bite.
Love is a funny thing, just like a lizard,
It curls up 'round your heart and then jumps into your gizzard.
Love is swell, it's so enticing,
It's orange gel, it's strawberry icing,
It's chocolate mousse, it's roasted goose,
It's ham on rye, it's banana pie.
Love's all good things without a question;
In other words, it's indigestion.

Although the poem sounded cute and I could always count on it to bring the response I anticipated, I knew that on the inside I was wishing the opposite to be true. Every teenager who laughed did so because it was "cool" to make fun of something you knew so little about. Only when it became something real did we know that hearts are built and torn on this thing called love.

Another poem went this way:

Slippery ice, very thin,
Pretty girl tumbles in,
Saw a boy on the bank,
Gave a shriek, then she sank.
Boy on hand, heard her shout,
Jumped right in, pulled her out.

Now she's his, very nice.

But she had to break the ice.

With all of its frivolity and lightheartedness, this poem, too, brings a smile because we all remember the first time we set eyes on the one who attracted us this way. It is easy for a young man to imagine a moment of gallantry when by some daring act of courage he rescues a girl—whether it be from slippery ice or a burning building—who turns out to be the lovely young girl of his dreams, and he whisks her off to safety. That alone, he thinks to himself, would prompt her parents to say, "That man deserves your love."

That word, *love*, is probably one of the most used and abused epithets that mankind has ever pondered. It has brought peace to many and yet, misunderstood and distorted, has broken many. And as you and I begin to look at this theme, I want to particularly challenge you who are unmarried with certain principles that the Bible gives us. These truths are undeniable if you are to build a successful home. If you are well on your journey in marriage, these thoughts, I trust, will light a fresh fire and bring your commitment back to where God intended it to be. Any human being who violates the laws of God only ends up proving them, not destroying them. The Word of God remains eternal. Those who have tried to bury it only find out that the Bible rises up to outlive its pallbearers.

The first book of the Old Testament, the Book of Genesis, speaks of our roots. It begins with the words, "In the beginning God . . ." and ends with the words, "So Joseph died and was buried." I find that fascinating. The book starts with the creating God and ends with a man in a coffin. In those first few words, "In the beginning God . . ." lies the paradigm of how everything in this world of time and space began. God, in His power, brought it to be. I think it was Dr. Billy Graham who once said, "I have no problem believing that the whale swallowed Jonah. I would have even believed it if Jonah had swallowed the whale." If you will pardon the pun, that is not flippant gullibility. That is the defining truth that underlies whether the supernatural is part and parcel of our lives or just a pipe dream. A. W. Tozer said, "Give me Genesis 1:1, and the rest of the Bible poses no problem for me." Once you accept the reality of God as not merely an assumption but the undeniable foundation of our very lives, many other deductions for life follow.

The distinguished philosopher Mortimer Adler, who was co-editor of *The Great Books of the Western World,* was once asked a very obvious question. This compilation of books contains essays on every major subject addressed by Western thinkers over the centuries. The longest article is on God. When an interviewer asked Adler why this was so, he replied, "More consequences for life and action follow from the affirmation or denial of God than from answering any other basic question."[1] Adler was absolutely right. The consequences of sacredness and profanity are worlds apart. If life is from God, then life is essentially sacred. If God is not necessary for life, then life is profane. The word *profane* means "outside the temple"—that is, God has no jurisdiction over life or part in it. "In the beginning God . . ." must be the generating dictum of all our choices and commitments.

From the beginning God positioned this relationship of man and woman in a unique context. Having created Adam, God said, "It is not good for the man to be alone" (Genesis 2:18), so He created a partner for him. Man's aloneness was an impediment to his complete fulfillment. I find that to be thought provoking, because in a very real sense man was not alone. God was with him. Adam experienced companionship in his relationship with God. God walked and talked with him. Their communion was nestled in the beauty of a garden. Yet God said that man was "alone." Interestingly, He made this pronouncement before Adam's disobedience ruptured his relationship with God. So when God says, "It is not good for the man to be alone," He must have had in mind a kind of companionship uniquely human to help meet Adam's human finitude in a way that God designed and orchestrated. In other words, God has made each of us with certain needs that are an intrinsic part of being human—needs that only a fellow human being can meet. We must step back and take note of that. Once we understand this, we realize that though God uses marriage to *represent* His relationship with us, the Church, that relationship with God is not identical to marriage. God has designed marriage to be a distinctly human relationship, different from all others. That is the first reminder in the creation of humanity.

THE BASIS ESTABLISHED

There is another reality that is often forgotten. When God said that it was not good for the man to be alone, even though he was in a close relationship with God, He created a woman. The fact that God did not create another man ought not to escape our attention. The companionship and the complementariness in that created pattern is defining for all of the rest of procreation. The woman met the desire, the need, and the insufficiency of the man in a way that God precluded Himself from and that another man was not intended to meet. Neither the gender of maleness nor the man's spiritual relationship with his heavenly Father was to provide this particular relationship.

Let me describe this in another way, in order to reinforce it. In Himself, God is all in all. There is nothing He lacks in His perfection. He is wholly sufficient for all our needs, yet He chose to craft a relationship designed so specifically that only a woman could complete the incompleteness of the man. It is the distinctive role of a woman, fashioned and splendidly made, to meet a need that could not be fulfilled by another man. This is an extraordinary order in creation made by God to "perfect" the entity He called Adam. The language reveals this: It is not just "the man"; it is now "the man *and* his wife" (Genesis 3:8; emphasis added).

G. K. Chesterton was once asked what one book he would want to have in his possession if he were stranded on an island. *How to Build a Boat,* came his immediate answer. Here in the garden, a magnificently designed companion completes the text on *How to Live in a Garden.*

According to the Scriptures, when Adam saw her, he said, "This is now bone of my bones and flesh of my flesh; she shall be called 'woman,' for she was taken out of man" (Genesis 2:23). She is part of him yet distinct from him. She is dissimilar in her physical makeup but complementary in her spirit. The man and the woman have a created distinction with an implicit codependence. The puzzle of the man's aloneness is solved by the "forming and shaping" of the woman. In that perfect fit, the picture God designed is complete. I have purposely belabored this point because this design and supremacy of relationship has been maligned in our culture, which mangles male-female relationships. The entire fury over gender warfare and sexuality is because the issues are positioned purely in pragmatic terms, forgetting that in the first created order there was specific design and intended purpose. All the philosophizing and arguing by well-meaning people to the contrary will not explain why the biology is so distinctive, as is the chemistry that follows. The differences between men and women are not perfunctory; they are essential. The complementariness is not bestowed by society; it is God-given. The purpose is not just love; it is procreation. It is not merely a provision; it is a pattern. Woman is not a fellow man; she is a unique entity, part of man but separate from him. The difference matters and is sacred in purpose. In violating this we violate a transcending intent.

Philosopher Peter Kreeft, commenting on Francis Bacon's *Man's Conquest of Nature,* had this to say: "The term in the phrase Man's conquest of Nature is a sexually chauvinistic term, not because all use of the traditional generic 'Man' is, but because we have a civilization that is in the midst of what Karl Stern called 'the flight from woman.' We extol action over being, analysis over intuition, problems over mysteries, success over contentment, conquering over nurturing, the quick fix over life-long commitments, the prostitute over the mother."[2]

Kreeft goes on to remind us that Aristotle gave three reasons for seeking knowledge: truth, moral action, and power or the ability to make things (technology or technique). Francis Bacon and our modern pragmatists, says Kreeft, have inverted the reasons. Truth and morality are displaced by our desire to make things in our own image.

This flight from womanhood is the costly price we have paid in our gender wars by making *difference* synonymous with *hierarchy.*

God made the differences, and those differences are purposeful. There is also difference in the Trinity without inferiority.

In human terms, romance, marriage, sexual consummation, and commitment became the very fabric of society. There is a primacy of relationship that is ascribed the ultimate commitment in human terms. The exclusive nature of the commitment between the man and the woman is made in a most profound pronouncement by God Himself: "For this reason a man will leave his father and mother and be united to his wife, and they will become one flesh" (Genesis 2:24). God designed marriage for union and communion. Adam and Eve had no mother or father to leave, but they were now to become father and mother and transfer the trust so that as God had made them separate yet one, marriage would continue from generation to generation.

This was the first home. This was the first family. From here, all of humanity emerged. The home was instituted before the Church was brought into being. May I underscore that God intended the home to be the seed from which culture flowers and history unfolds. It is not coincidental that a garden was the first setting for the first home.

Looking at the average home today, we see how much heartache has resulted because we no longer see marriage God's way. We seem to be living more in a wilderness, isolated from one another. Self-centeredness and personal ambition have replaced the love of a man for a woman and the raising of the family. The seeds of selfishness have given root to the thorns and hurts of fractured families. If our homes fail, history collapses.

Five thousand years ago, Abraham saw the need to preserve his children and their descendants. Concerned about the generation to come and claiming the promise of God, he called upon his trusted servant and said, "I want you to help me in this. Would you follow these instructions and find the woman whom my son Isaac, this chosen seed, should marry?" (see Genesis 24:3).

Those of us living in the West will have difficulty understanding some of these concepts, but I will try to delineate how they hold true as a moral basis, whether East or West. We make a mistake in thinking that something is right or wrong because our culture deems it such. Nothing could be further from the truth. Yes, culture may approve or disapprove, but if there is no overarching umbrella of truth beyond culture, our times may wreak havoc in the name of culture. Slavery is a classic example of this. People did not flinch at the barbarous practice that was tolerated for so long, the ramifications of which are with us to this day. The abuse of marriage is no less a crime against humanity.

In Abraham's time, there was a very real assumption in the mix of religion and societal interaction that the parents played a pivotal role in making the decision about whom their child would marry. Over time, this practice has been abused and the child often becomes the victim. But in the ideal sense, parental counsel was intended to be a voice of love and wisdom that could keep a young life from being swept away by the insincere guile of a suitor.

THE VOICE IS JUST NOT OUR OWN

Abraham sent Eliezer to search for a bride from the land of his own beginnings. This is the first major fact that emerges. Isaac was not the only one involved in this selection process, and I think that's pivotal. God was concerned. Abraham had prayed. Eliezer was sent. A trusted servant and a devoted father played a vital part in the selection of the bride.

We run into a mental debate within ourselves at this point. You see, when you or I first set our eyes upon the one whom we think we have always wanted and the heartbeat of romance begins to pound, we are very susceptible to many dangerous situations. Our emotions can take over and prevent our minds from functioning with legitimate objectivity. In our minds, our parents can become merely interrupters of a relationship rather than wise guides helping us find the right person.

Before you completely dismiss that warning, think about it—first as a child and then as a potential parent who one day will guide your own child in making the same decision. Young people, be immensely careful when you pledge your life to somebody if your parents are not in sympathy with your decision—particularly if your parents love God.

In my own personal experience I found this principle extremely difficult to apply when the test came. The struggle to honor this commitment to our parents was a deep one because of the unique situation in which we found ourselves. I came from one part of the world, born and raised in India. The girl I loved came from another part of the world, Canada, and when we first met and developed an interest in each other, none of our parents supported our relationship for various reasons. We knew this would be a mountain to scale if we were to ever see the light of their consent and blessing.

So I found myself in this emotionally weighty situation, wondering to what degree I was going to follow this singularly important guiding principle in our friendship. As much as there was a struggle within my soul, I had told Margie that if our parents, who dearly loved our heavenly Father, were not supportive of our relationship, there was no way I could seek the blessing of God upon us. Margie and I made this a matter of passionate prayer. We talked, we prayed, we wept, and we struggled. A love I wanted was potentially going to be taken from me. This commitment to receiving our parents' blessing became an important proving ground in our relationship.

I fully realize that there are many contingencies that come into play in the issue of parental blessing. There are many questions that one may raise. Parental blessing is a highly desired ideal but cannot be considered in a vacuum. In our day and age, one may argue both for and against. Times have changed, cultures are now intermixed, and travel is prolific.

Interestingly enough, on a recent visit to India, a journalist asked me during an interview what I thought of common-law relationships. Quite surprised at this question in the context of India, I asked her why she asked it. "Because it has become very common here," she said. Our world has changed in massive proportions from the world of a generation ago. More and more young people have economic and emotional independence from their parents, and as a result, they are making life choices—such as living together outside of marriage—without their parents' input.

While not a guarantee, parental counsel and blessing is nevertheless the way of wisdom and must be seriously considered. While ideals are beacons that guide us, they do not always present themselves in ideal fashion. Parents must be certain that they are not trying to relive their lives through their children, and children must be certain that they are not dishonoring their parents with a dishonest self-justification.

The famed John Wesley, who preached and taught two continents into a powerful revival, nevertheless went against the wisdom offered by many in his choice for a wife. He paid a bitter price for having done so. He himself would have testified that his marriage was a colossal blunder, the biggest mistake of his life. All I can say is that the joy of receiving the blessing of both parents keeps the heart in tune with the spirit and makes the joy complete in this huge step forward.

One must be profoundly responsible when categorically presenting an absolute, so let me put it this way. *The chances are that if you marry somebody in violation of your parents' will, you are playing a high-stakes game as you enter the future. Any time you violate an authority that has been put in place by God, you need to be twice as sure you are doing the right thing.*

That's as carefully as I can state it.

2

THE WILL TO DO

If the will is to be resurrected,
it must first go to the Cross.

✠

I have heard it said that the longest journey in life is from the head to the heart. Another way to say the same thing is that the spirit is willing but the flesh is weak. Yet another aphorism of our time is that beginning well is a momentary thing; finishing well is a lifelong thing. All of these point to one reality—our knowledge and our response are not always in keeping with each other. We seem to be inclined to separate what God intended to remain joined together.

Solomon proved this centuries ago. He made a fascinating statement in the Book of Ecclesiastes. He relates all the areas in which he searched for meaning—pleasure, riches, power, fame, and everything else one could imagine. Through all of these forays in a search for fulfillment, he says, "My wisdom stayed with me" (Ecclesiastes 2:9). How is that possible, we ask, when his day-to-day life was a colossal mess? I understand him to mean that in the midst of his duplicity, his theoretical knowledge of right and wrong never left him. He knew how to discern. But he was volitionally weak and unable to resist the tug of attraction into wrong behavior.

I have shared the following story many times over the years. Those from parts of the world where this is foreign shake their heads in disbelief, wondering how this can even be theoretically plausible, let alone practically workable. But read the reasoning first and then I will try to explain.

I give you an example of my older brother, who lives in Toronto, Canada. The story dates back to the late 1960s. At that time he was a systems engineer with IBM. Since that time, he has gone on to do several very impressive things in the world of computer software. In other words, he is mentally all right. He doesn't have any major problem as far as his IQ is concerned. I say that because you may begin to wonder as I tell his story.

When he was in his mid-twenties, my brother came to my father and said, "You know, Dad, I've always maintained even when we were in India that I'm only going to marry the girl you choose for me. I guess I am ready now. Would you please begin a search for a girl for me to marry?"

I really didn't believe he'd go through with it. We were living in Toronto, thousands of miles and a cultural planet away from the land of our birth. But this was his choice. He wanted my parents to help in "The Search." My father and mother said, "Fine. Tell us the kind of young woman you're looking for." My brother gave his "ideal partner" speech and proceeded to describe the kind of person he would choose to marry.

Under normal circumstances, the parents would travel around and look for somebody that met the criteria, but in this instance my brother said to our father, "Look, you really don't need to do that. Why don't you just write to your sister in Bombay and let her do the groundwork? We'll just correspond back and forth and take it from there."

Thus began his quest and what I called our family entertainment hour every night around the table. My father wrote to his sister, and in response came numerous letters with suggestions, photographs, and information sheets ad nauseam. Oh! The jokes that would fly! The unsolicited advice from every member of the family was profuse. The sarcasm, wondering whether this poor woman had the faintest clue of his shortcomings! (From my experience with photographs I have learned that if you find a good photographer and pay him enough, he can make anybody look splendid. One of the first things people do when you arrive for a speaking event is to compare the reality with your publicity photograph. Many times they can probably say, "Twenty years ago he may have looked like that, but now . . .")

Pictures can tell an awful lot that's really not there. The camera can and does lie. But my brother would sit in his bed at night and look over all those pictures, study the lists of accomplishments and qualifications, and say, "What do you think of this one, Rav? Isn't she lovely? Look at the description. She's even the church organist." I could not resist pointing out how important a feature that was for a successful marriage.

He narrowed the "applicants" to a short list and, finally focusing on one person, began to correspond with her. Then they advanced to telephone conversations, but not many because that was "too expensive." One could tell that reality was closing in. Finally, believe it or not, they both felt this was it. The dates for the engagement and the marriage were set with these two never having met.

My brother and my father flew from Toronto to Bombay. More than one thousand wedding invitations were sent before my brother and his bride-to-be had ever seen each other. Two days after his arrival was the engagement date and a day or so later was the wedding date. He would then bring his bride back to Canada, all within a week, and they would live "happily ever after." That, at any rate, was the plan.

I thought to myself, *Oh my! You know, this is faith. Maybe it is even less than that. This is credulity!* I began to get really concerned, so before my brother left for Bombay, I mustered up the courage to caution him. I said, "I don't want to challenge anything you're doing, but I do have a brief question. What are you going to do when you arrive in Bombay, come down the Jetway and see a young woman standing there with a garland in her hand, and say to yourself, *Good grief! I hope that's not her. I hope that's somebody else!* Or she looks at you and thinks to herself, *I hope that's not him. I hope that's his brother!* What on earth will you do? Are you going to take her aside, talk it over, and then make an announcement saying, 'We have met . . . we will not be proceeding with our plans'? Will you get on the telephone or write letters to everybody and say, 'Folks, we've met. The wedding is off.'"

My brother just stared at me. He said, "Are you through?" I told him that for the moment I was just awaiting his answer. Then he said something that was absolutely defining for him: "Write this down, and don't ever forget it: Love is as much a question of the will as it is of the emotion. And if you will to love somebody, you can."

That statement brought our conversation to a sudden stop. That was thirty-five years ago. My brother and his wife now have three children and make their home in Toronto. Has it been easy? No. Marriage never is easy. But the challenges they face do not come from an absence of commitment.

The statement "If you will to love somebody, you can" has the ring of truth, but deep inside we wonder, *How does one "will"?* It is a little bit like ordering somebody to love you. How does one go beyond the discernment to the practice? If knowledge does not guarantee behavior, where does one go to translate the prerequisite into action? Can it really be done?

A FALSE START

The first thing to bear in mind is that we exaggerate the separation of the emotion and the will as two distinct faculties of operation—some kind of misshapen two-headed monster. Think, for example, of the caricature we make of one difference between men and women. We seem to think that women are more emotionally driven and men more cerebrally driven. If that caricature were true, why is it that more men fall into infidelity after marriage than do women? If women are more emotionally driven, should it not be the other way around? I think it more appropriate to say that women in general recognize the emotional *ramifications* of their acts better than men do. Men *do* feel emotion, but they do so selectively and fail to face the consequences of reality. Betray a man and you find out that his emotions surge to the top. I believe that a legitimate understanding of what is happening here can preserve the grand union between emotion and will.

Without the will, marriage is a mockery; without emotion, it is a drudgery. You need both.

We like the side dealing with emotion, not the will. I have now been married more than thirty years. I often look back at the time when I was on the other side of the marital line and remember how I thought about marriage then. One particular conversation stands out. A year before I was married, I was sitting in a Christian education class when the professor quite dramatically started to philosophize about life. Commenting on the home, he said, "I want you students to know that love is hard work."

I leaned over to my classmate and whispered, "I wouldn't want to be married to anybody who goes around telling everybody how hard it is to love me."

He said, "I agree with you. Why don't you ask him about it?" Like a fool, I did.

I stood up and said, "Excuse me, sir . . . I am not quite comfortable with your categorization of love as 'hard work.'"

The professor stared at me, evidently not taking too kindly to my challenge, and demanded, "Zacharias, are you married?"

When I responded, "No, sir," he said, "Then why don't you just be quiet and sit down? You don't have a clue what you are talking about." I sat down.

One year later I was married. After being married all these years, I can unblushingly say, he was right. Love *is* hard work. I would carry it one step further. It is the hardest work I know of, work from which you are never entitled to take a vacation. You take on burdens and cares. You inherit problems. You have to feel beyond yourself. You have to think of things other than yourself.

Your responsibilities are now multiplied, and you are trusted with greater commitments.

You see, the easiest part of our marriage was the wedding ceremony. I remember arriving at the church early. I could hardly wait. As the church filled with guests and the appropriate music was played for the ceremony to begin, I turned to see my bride enter the sanctuary. No, I did not think of all the weddings I had gate-crashed or of all the ceremonies I had witnessed. This was not someone else's wedding; this was a special moment for us. It was one of the most ecstatic feelings the human heart could ever endure. There is no word in the English dictionary to describe it except the word *Wow!* It was the crystallization of my every romantic dream. That which was once far off was now near. That which I longed for was now in hand.

As Margie came up the aisle to join me at the front of the church, my heart was in a flutter. So much so that when the minister told me in old English to "salute the bride," out of sheer nervousness I was on the verge of literally saluting her. There is nothing so magnificent as a beautiful, blushing bride behind a veil that cannot hide the radiant glow of a dream coming true. If the flutter of a heart were all that one needs to fly, the groom would soar to celestial heights. No! The groom does not need to soar at that moment, for God Himself comes near and says, *This is My precious gift to you. Receive it with reverence and guard it with diligence.*

The ceremony was followed by the reception. What a wonderful way to celebrate with friends. At the end of the reception we drove to the honeymoon capital of North America—Niagara Falls—where we stayed for the night at Michael's Inn. (Thankfully, Michael wasn't.) From there it was on to Cape Cod, Massachusetts. I remember carrying her over the threshold. My heart was as full as I had hoped it would be. I had an overwhelming sense of gallantry as I carried her into the room.

At about two o'clock in the morning, Margie got up. I thought, *Surely the honeymoon couldn't be over already . . . where is she going?* So I asked, "Where are you going, honey?" She answered, "I'm going to get a glass of water." I said, "Stay right here, I'll get it for you." That was May 6, 1972. I was thrilled to get up at two o'clock in the morning and get her a glass of water. My! What sacrifice!

But five years go by. Someone has wryly quipped, "Sacrifice in America is when the electric blanket doesn't work." So one night I find myself comfortably tucked in bed, and about two or three o'clock, I hear the rustle of the sheets. She's getting up again, and the temptation is to pull the covers over my face and cease to hear anything at that moment—for at least one reason. She looked different. You see, on May 6, 1972, she looked grand. Absolutely grand! But five years later, she had some funny things in her hair at night that generally prompted one question, "What stations are you able to get under that influence?" I have been chided for that remark many times so I should add that she no longer wears them.

Times have changed. But I do recall that sight. Somehow the first word that leaped into my mind was not the word *Wow!* But I still do the right thing, because the tug of love is a commitment stronger than merely the flutter of the heart.

Chivalry in love has nothing to do with the sweetness of the appearance. It has everything to do with the tenderness of a heart determined to serve. That is the first hard lesson to learn. You do not act under the impetus of charm but out of a commitment to make someone's life the joy you want it to be. In the early days of marriage, joy precedes the act. Tragically, as the years go by joy can be severed from the act until finally, the act itself is no more. This ought not to be. Over time it is the companionship that brings joy, and service is the natural outworking of the joy of commitment. Failure to act kills it.

William Doherty begins his excellent book *Take Back Your Marriage* with a powerful illustration. His office is located in St. Paul, Minnesota, not far from the farthest point north on the Mississippi River. He describes the river's formidable but silent current that drives its waters southward. "Everything on the water that is not powered by wind, gasoline, or human muscle" heads south. Then he adds these words: "I have thought that getting married is like launching a canoe into the Mississippi at St. Paul. If you don't paddle, you go south. No matter how much you love each other, no matter how full of hope and promise and good intentions, if you stay on the Mississippi without a good deal of paddling—occasional paddling is not enough—you end up in New Orleans. Which is a problem if you want to stay north."[1]

But this kind of commitment does not come easily. Only if it is taken seriously does it become a sheer delight of the heart. I will also add that this kind of commitment is not seen much in the times in which we live. The reason we have a crisis in our gender relationships is not that we are culturally indoctrinated but that we would rather be served than serve. We would rather be the head than the feet. The Christian faith stands unique in pointing out that the Son of Man came to seek and to save that which was lost. The Son of Man came to serve. This means that the service He gave to humanity was given even when we least merited that sacrifice. There is a joy in service that transcends emotional temporariness.

A Realistic Picture

An act, especially of such magnitude as marriage, must be thoughtfully considered before it becomes an act. Impulsive acts die impulsive deaths. This works both ways, in honoring that which is right and in resisting that which is wrong. Always make the decision before the emotion stirs you into wrongheaded commitments. We refer to people as impulse buyers. That is not a good way to buy. Step back, measure the value of what you are getting, and then buy it. This applies a thousandfold more in marriage. Don't be deceived by the flutter of the heart. Love is a commitment that will be tested in the most vulnerable areas of spirituality, a commitment that will force you to make some very difficult choices. It is a commitment that demands that you deal with your lust, your greed, your pride, your power, your desire to control, your temper, your patience, and every area of temptation that the Bible so clearly talks about. It demands the quality of commitment that Jesus demonstrates in His relationship to us.

Jesus said that greater love has no man than to lay down his life for his friend. But it is probably more difficult to *live* a life of continual dying to oneself than to die in one moment. Marriage is hard work, and that's why, when you come to that pivotal moment of decision, my suggestion is that you seek the advice of somebody you love and respect. Don't make such a decision on your own just because you have romantic feelings. Seek out the wisdom of your minister, the wisdom of your parents, and the wisdom of friends, and realize that romance has to be transcended by a strong will and a degree of commitment to you and by you. The important thing to bear in mind is that you must face your willingness to die to yourself before you choose to walk down the aisle. Is this person the one for whom you are willing to die daily? Is this person to whom you say, "I do" also the one for whom you are willing to say, "No, I don't" to everybody else? Be assured that marriage will cost you everything.

I recall a young couple who came to me for premarital counseling. They looked so much in love and cherished each other. But as I administered a premarital test to see where their expectations and hopes matched or differed, something very startling emerged. They disclosed to me that the young man had tragically contracted a deadly disease some time back, a disease that would also make intimacy precarious. Only in his twenties, he was facing death within two to three years. As we talked, they were obviously struggling with whether it was the right thing to be married or whether they should just let this dream die. Their love was deep, and they were willing to face even a short wedded life to have the delight of those few years. Many asked them to think it through carefully.

My counsel to them was simply this: Think it over, because the person you are now and the person you will be when you have to say your final parting will not be the same. You will have to change and work at sacrificial expressions in such a way that it will not be just your names that will change but your very being. Each of you will have a part of the other in your emotions and in your thinking so that you change for the sake of the other. Can you face the aloneness when he is gone and then find it possible to love another with a part of this person ever in your soul? Will you want to go through it all over again? Think about it, because you will be giving huge portions of yourself over a short period.

I could not fight off the tears when I heard their decision, although their reasoning was sound. They both knew that to marry would entail an emotional component that would put them on the edge, right from the beginning. When the time came for him to depart, her life would also have been spent emotionally, though she would still be young. Recognizing the emotional cost of saying yes, they chose the path of saying no to conserve the power of her youth and save it for someone else who in the long run would merit that total investment of her life. They chose to give up their dream of marriage but remained very close friends.

To many of us this story may seem sad, but it is the lesson of the will. If you are to learn to control the will, you must harness it early in any battle. Lines must be drawn not at the level of acting but at the level of thinking. Lines must be drawn not at the level of doing but at the level of desiring. Lines must be drawn not at the level of contact but at the level of sight. Lines must be drawn knowing that marriage is not just a condition of being but a condition of becoming. The two become one, but the becoming is both a moment and a process.

STEADYING THE WILL

How do you harness the will? First, by recognizing that dying to yourself is an act of the will. You must choose to lay down your life in the best sense of the term. You surrender your will to the will of God by an act of commitment and in the power of the indwelling of the Holy Spirit of God. That is the indispensable beginning. No one likes to begin life with a funeral. But in a sense, that is where marriage begins. You choose to die to yourself and to bring to life a new affection.

The famed Scottish preacher Thomas Chalmers once preached an unforgettable sermon titled "The Expulsive Power of a New Affection." While his theme was conversion, the implications are similar for marital commitment. An affection of such force takes charge that it expels other affections that are inimical to this one. That is the first step—dying to yourself.

There is no greater illustration of marriage and of the appropriate action to take when it is in trouble than the story of the prophet Hosea. A pastor, Hosea married a woman who sold herself into prostitution. Even the names of their three children illustrated the pain of this broken home. But the remarkable thing is that while Hosea's wife was still in her lifestyle of prostitution God commanded him to buy her back. Even more remarkable and difficult was the rest of God's command to Hosea: "Go, show your love to your wife again" (Hosea 3:1).

We see it here clearly. Love is a command, not just a feeling. Somehow, in the romantic world of music and theater we have made love to be what it is not. We have so mixed it with beauty and charm and sensuality and contact that we have robbed it of its higher call of cherishing and nurturing. Watch two young people in a passionate embrace—it may be love, but it may also be nothing more than passion. Watch two elderly people walking hand in hand with evident concern for each other, and you are closer to seeing love in that relationship than in the youthful embrace.

G. K. Chesterton said these powerful words: "They have invented a phrase, a phrase that is a black and white contradiction in two words—'free love'—as if a lover ever had been, or ever could be, free. It is the nature of love to bind itself, and the institution of marriage merely paid the average man the compliment of taking him at his word."[2]

This brings into focus an element of the will. The will is that faculty which can only be tested when pain is as much a part of its choice as pleasure is. Let me state it another way. The will is that disposition of the mind that will choose a path and bind itself with love, even if pain is mixed with the choice. In the West, particularly, we have become so resistant to pain that at the slightest hint of it, we prepare to flee by some shortcut or some solution that masks the discomfort.

By His example, Jesus teaches us the opposite. Think back to the scene we find within the pages of the Gospels when Jesus was about to be tried and crucified. He struggled with the agony of being separated from His Father and of bearing the entire weight of human sin. None of us will ever know what that felt like, but we know what it is to bear a small portion of sin's weight and feel crushed by it.

During the days of my undergraduate studies in India, I remember an incident that to this day brings a negative response within me. We were in the midst of a class when the professor asked the student in front of me to answer a question. The student stood to his feet, presented his answer, and as he was about to sit down, the student next to me covertly slid the stool out from under him with his foot. I only had a fraction of a second to reach out and try to push the stool back into place so that the young man would not land on the floor with a terrible, possibly injurious jolt. But I couldn't do it fast enough and the student fell hard.

The professor had only seen my hand trying to reach the stool and assumed that I had pulled it out from under him. Without any discussion, he ordered me out of the class. I got as far as saying, "But sir . . ." before he interrupted me and said, "I don't want any explanation for such a shameful act. Just get out of my class." The boy who had actually done it sat quietly and said nothing while both the boy who fell and the professor thought it was I who had done it. Others who had watched it all happen thought they had better stay out of it for fear of some reprisal. In short, I bore the wrong of another person and to this day am rankled by the memory.

That is a small, minute thing in the light of what I say to you. When Jesus took, by His own will, the guilt of the world upon

Himself, knowing the agony of separation from the Father that would follow because the Father would have to treat Him as the guilty one, He cried out to His Father, "If it is Your will, take this cup away from Me" (Luke 22:42 NKJV). He did not want to taste the bitterness of human sin, the greatest consequence of which was separation from God the Father. But then He also cried, "Nevertheless not My will, but Yours, be done" (v. 42 NKJV).

I wonder what I would have done if a third student, in order to protect me, had stood up and taken the blame? I would have found it unfathomable, but an act for which I would have surrendered much in order to express my heartfelt gratitude. You see, the will is always in a dramatic clash with other wills, including our own wishes. Fear, self-protection, indifference—numerous emotions and concerns test the will and often lead us astray. At the moment my will is tested to do wrong, it must remember the price that was paid on my behalf by the One who took the punishment for my will. By that act, He invited me to die to my own will, having received the gift of being accepted by Him, which my will alone could not have made possible.

In exchange, I receive the will of God by which to live and find delight. Nothing brings harmony more than embracing the will of God. Nothing brings fragmentation more than turning away from the will of God. *Marriage is the harmony of God synchronizing two wills with the will of the Father.* When that happens, the heart resounds with the feeling, even though it involves sacrifice.

Marriages are broken when even one of the two wills breaks from the will of the Father. When that happens the heart is broken as well, even though there is a path that may seem to provide an easier way out. That is when God takes over. Unless I understand the Cross, I cannot understand why my commitment to what is right must take precedence over what I prefer. Your marriage, as your conversion, begins at the Cross. Only then does the resurrection follow.

When my younger brother was about seven years old, he contracted double pneumonia and typhoid fever. As each day came and went, his condition deteriorated and the doctors said there was little chance of him recovering. Our entire family moved out of our home to live with my aunt while my mom was living in the hospital with my brother.

I recall going to visit him in the hospital one evening. He was not expected to survive the night. He looked absolutely pathetic, shriveled to a bundle of bones. But something happened that night as we were to find out later. All of us, except my mother, left the hospital not expecting to see him again. But my mother spent the night by his bedside, reaching out and touching his face or stroking his head. As the night wore on, out of sheer exhaustion she fell asleep in her chair. Night after night she had stayed awake, yet on this night, his last night, she had run out of strength. Her head drooped and she fell asleep for a couple of hours—the very hours she was told he would die.

She awakened with a start to find him still alive. In fact, she felt a warmth to his body she had not felt before. As one day passed into another, he became stronger until he had fully recovered.

My mother told us often that she felt that when she had given all she had to give and could give no more, God had taken over and given her the sleep she so needed as He restored the ailing frame of her son. This, to me, is a remarkable expression of will and hope. The rest of the family was comfortably asleep at home. The one whose heart was most entwined with his young life, by sheer sacrifice and self-denial, worked for his well-being until she could do nothing else but stay close, and that's when God took over.

When your will is committed to God, He carries you when all else seems spent, to rescue what you had invested by your dedication.

A few days ago, while writing this chapter in a small Asian city, I took an early morning walk and saw two workmen who were dismantling a cement block wall, taking great care to keep the blocks intact for another structure they were building. What a metaphor this is for the home! When two lives meet, they are like two distinct walls. Each has to start by dismantling his or her wall one brick at a time, and then those bricks are taken intact and with other materials used to build a structure with a roof that brings them together at the top. That is the new home. Two wills are as two walls. Rightly dismantled and rebuilt they provide the strength for a new union of two lives.

The playwright Thornton Wilder said it well: "I didn't marry you because you were perfect. I didn't even marry you because I loved you. I married you because you gave me a promise. That promise made up for your faults. And the promise I gave you made up for mine. Two imperfect people got married and it was the promise that made the marriage. And when our children were growing up, it wasn't a house that protected them; and it wasn't our love that protected them—it was that promise."[3]

3

THE LIVING ACT
OF A DEAD SELF

*Kindness is the coinage of investment
with the returns reaped in personality.*

I f the first thing about committing the will is that it is a death to yourself, what comes to life is a disposition that seeks to serve. The one who serves does so with kindness and gentleness. This is something we almost never think of anymore, that we are called to the service of love. We are so prone to lay claim to our rights that we bury the demand that calls us to serve. Our love story shows us in a simple act the beauty of service that has at its heart a kind spirit.

Rebekah emerges to me as a lovely woman. I doubt you and I have ever given much thought to how much a camel drinks. I suspect it would have been a significant time commitment to give just one camel its load of drink for the day. This young woman said, "You rest awhile, sir. I'll not only give you the water, I will take care of your camels, too—all ten of them." The thoughtfulness and kindness she demonstrated are exemplary. Her actions could not have been typical because they served as a sign to Eliezer.

One of the privileges of traveling and visiting different cultures is the opportunity of entering different homes—and observing much. One impression of any relationship that stands out and is remembered is the level of kindness or unkindness demonstrated between a husband and wife. The first is refreshing; the latter is discomforting. I would go so far as to say that there is never a reason to be unkind. There may be reasons to disagree. There may be reasons to struggle. After all, two wills are merging into one. There are constant compromises and surrenders demanded, but there is never a reason to be unkind, particularly when you are tampering with the very fragile nature of a person's sensitivities. I have seen love maimed and even killed by unkind words. Unkindness can be the hatpin to the heart of love and bleed it to death. Lives and dispositions are much more fragile than we think. Every relationship should be marked "Fragile: Handle with Care."

In our marriage I have prayed constantly that God will so fill Margie and me with His presence that even in some of the difficult moments we may have to work through, we may be able to resist the temptation to be rude or unkind to each other. I like to use the term *cherishing* your partner. That word comes from the French verb *chérir,* which means to hold dear or endear to yourself, to care for tenderly, to esteem or consider a person costly by your treatment of him or her. What you cherish, you hold close to you; what you hold closely, you protect; what you protect, you have. "To have and to hold" can be reversed to say "to hold and to have." This is very much rooted in the very terms God uses of His own kindness to His people.

THE HEART AND THE HANDS

From the time the story begins, there are two themes repeated with frequency. The first is the covenantal term for God's love, His *hesed* or "loving-kindness." *Hesed* is the unmerited and generous favor of God. It is a love that is gentle and always reaching out to the object of that love. This is the protection that Abraham experienced as God reached out to him, and this loving-kindness from God caused him to serve others. This loving-kindness is exemplified in the way Isaac received his bride-to-be.

Old Testament scholar Daniel Block describes *hesed* as "that quality that moves a person to act for the benefit of another without respect to the advantage that it might bring to the one who expresses it.... [This] quality is expressed fundamentally in action rather than word or emotion."[1] That is very well put. It is an attribute that puts the other first and is defined by action rather than by emotion. It is interesting that in English we must put two words together in order to get the concept of the one word *hesed*—loving-kindness.

You may recall that in the Greek language there are four words for the English word *love*—*agape,* meaning a love that is pure enough to be used even of God; *phileo,* the love of friendship; *storge,* protective love, best described as the love of a parent for a child; and *eros,* romantic love. Marriage is the only relationship that blends all four loves. But it all has to begin with that loving-kindness, in the Old Testament intimated by the Hebrew word *hesed.* It is a term culturally laden with historic memory and collective hope. It is this love that has brought us this far and will carry us further. In the Old Testament God continually reminds His people of His *hesed.* It is the waiting and overflowing love that the prodigal son knew when he returned home and that the older son had forgotten by taking it for granted.

The Psalmist said, "Your love ["loving-kindness" in the King James Version] is better than life" (Psalm 63:3). One wonders how God's loving-kindness can be better than life when without life you cannot enjoy His loving-kindness. But the truth is that without God's loving-kindness, life is not worth living. In fact, that is precisely what David says as he begins Psalm 63:

> O God, you are my God,
>
>> earnestly I seek you;
>
> my soul thirsts for you,
>
>> my body longs for you,
>
> in a dry and weary land
>
>> where there is no water. . . .

Because your [loving-kindness] is better than life,

my lips will glorify you. (vv. 1, 3)

Parched lips do not sing, but a life that is full of love and refreshment does sing. Isaac and Rebekah had both experienced this *hesed*, this loving-kindness, and now in their meeting they knew it again. The Scriptures say ever so briefly but ever so pointedly of their meeting, ". . . he married Rebekah. So she became his wife, and he loved her" (Genesis 24:67). It is interesting to notice the sequence. We would have said he loved her and so she became his wife. Instead, the Scriptures tell us, "She became his wife, and he loved her."

Only a few verses later we are given a small glimpse into Isaac and Rebekah's private life when they were in another town and were unaware that they were being watched. The Bible says, "Abimelech . . . looked down from a window and saw Isaac caressing his wife Rebekah" (Genesis 26:8). That alone speaks volumes of his tenderness and affection toward her. In fact, the greatest compliment he paid her is given to us several years after they were married, when Isaac sent for their son Jacob, who was of marriageable age, and told him to go back to the family and home of Rebekah and look for a wife from within their extended family (see Genesis 28:1–2). That plea to his son lets us know that Isaac was certain he had done the right thing in marrying Rebekah, and it is a reminder again that the family from which one comes has great influence.

Translated into the daily routine it means this: There will be times in the relationship between a husband and wife when one says, "I'm feeling very unhappy, and I really can't even tell you what the reason is. All I know is that I need to be loved." There are times when no amount of talk, no explanation or solution to a situation can take the place of just being held in the arms of the person you love, of feeling loved and cared for. It's that kind of kindness, I think, that is able to walk the second mile.

Do you remember Jesus's illustration on that? In Jesus's time, the Roman yoke was literally and figuratively heavy upon the Jewish shoulder. The Jews resented the Romans for their power, their dominance, and their bullying of the Jewish people. They wanted a Messiah who would not only throw off the Roman yoke but would even bring tremendously punitive measures upon the Roman monarchy.

We can imagine a young Jewish man coming to Jesus one day and saying something like this: "The law in our land says that if a Roman soldier comes to me and asks me to carry his heavy arms and ammunition for him, I, as a Jew, must stop whatever else I am doing and walk with him one mile, carrying his burden. The next time he comes to me and demands that I carry his arms and ammunition just because I am a Jew, what should I say to him?"

Of course, the man was really hoping for some kind of answer that would encourage him to resist such domination.

But Jesus looked at him and said, "The next time he comes and asks you to walk with him one mile, at the end of the one mile pause and look into his eyes and say to him, 'Sir, would you mind if I carry it a second mile, also?'" (see Matthew 5:41). The counterperspective of Jesus Christ constantly left His questioners speechless because He moved love to its loftiest plane.

This principle is put to test early in the simpler things of life. May I illustrate one of those? I learned soon after being married that there is an unwritten law that says it is always the responsibility of the man of the house to carry out the garbage. I don't know where this idea came from, but no matter whose home you are in, it's always the man who takes out the garbage.

When we lived in Chicago during my days at graduate school, the garbage dump was at least fifty yards from our apartment. Chicago, of course, can get pretty windy and icy. It didn't seem to matter what the hour was, every time I went out of our apartment, my wife was always at the door to kiss me good-bye, which was fine. But it seemed that she always had a bag of garbage to hand me, even if I was headed out on a Friday night to begin a two-hundred-mile trip to preach.

What would you do? Like me, you would probably want to grab the garbage bag and say, "Here, give it to me!" Then muttering to yourself about the cruelty of life, you would go over to the garbage dump and jam the bag into the drums while the cats and dogs are pouncing all over the place; get into the car and slam the door, start the engine, and squeal the tires as you pull out of there; pull into the church parking lot, hurriedly put on your "Praise the Lord" face, stand behind the pulpit, and say, "Isn't it wonderful to be serving the Lord so willingly?"

No, no! That isn't what you do! Instead, you take the garbage bag ever so gently, so you don't hurt either her or the garbage. You take it in both arms as you slide across that miserable ice, whistling, "Everything is beautiful in its own way." Drop it into the drum very carefully. End of mile one!

Then you go back into your apartment—make sure she doesn't have a coronary now—and say, "Honey, I still have ten minutes to go. Would you like me to help you with the dishes before I leave?"

As far-fetched as that sounds, it is the coinage with which you make your investment of cherishing and caring. I do not know what mileage you have been asked to walk with your partner, but I have no doubt there is another mile you will still need to walk when things get tough. The Scriptures remind us, "Love is patient, love is kind" (1 Corinthians 13:4), and we should "consider how we may spur one another on toward love and good deeds" (Hebrews 10:24).

To the young woman I say, This is the moment in your life when he who is wooing you will be at his kindest. And if you do not see kindness in the man you are dating, beware! For the partnership you are looking for will be nourished and nurtured only on the basis of a love that is not arrogant or prideful, but kind.

There is a remote story in 1 Samuel, chapter 25, tucked in the middle of David's history. It begins as a touching episode but tapers off into disappointment for the ones involved. David is a young man at this time, fresh from gallant victories on the battlefield. Observing the need for some replenishment for his troops, he sends his soldiers to the home of a wealthy man named Nabal, who is married to a lovely young woman named Abigail.

David's message to Nabal is a plea. He reminds him that he has taken good care of his farmers during the war, and but for that protection, Nabal's wealth would have been plundered by the enemy. "Would you consider giving a love-offering to help feed my soldiers for the care they have given you?" asks David. No amount is stipulated; he just presents a fair request. But Nabal flatly turns down David's request, basically referring to him as a young "upstart" who credited himself with too much. David is angry at Nabal's response, perhaps justifiably, and decides to show Nabal who the real "upstart" is.

Up to this point in the story we have seen only the soldiers, David, and Nabal. But now there enters a unique woman, Abigail, Nabal's wife. She is informed of what has happened and could easily have said, "It serves my husband right for being such an idiot." But she doesn't play that game. Even though her husband does not merit her dignity and love, she does the honorable thing. She saddles up her donkeys with food and other goods and goes out to meet David, who is on his way to make short work of Nabal. When she comes face to face with David, she gives him a speech of a lifetime that goes something like this: "My husband's name is Nabal, and Nabal means 'fool.' Unfortunately, he has lived that way much of his life. But today, David, there is a bigger fool in the land, and that fool is you. You are planning to kill a man, but in doing so you will bring murder upon your own head. That will rob you of the enrichment with which God wants to bless you some day. Don't do it, David. Take what you please, but spare my husband."

David is absolutely silenced by Abigail's charm and wisdom. He tells her she can go on her way. She has accomplished her mission, and he will not harm Nabal.

One would think that was the end of the story. But unfortunately, it isn't. Impressed with Abigail's courage, wisdom, and poise, David was unable to get her out of his mind. She was an outstanding woman. As time went by, David heard that Nabal had died. His first thought was, *Aha! Abigail a widow! Maybe I can propose marriage to her.* And that is precisely what happened. She agreed and he married her.

But nothing is ever heard of Abigail again. It is as if he saw, he conquered . . . and that was it. The Scriptures go on to remind us of David's many wives and of his huge family in which sensuality reached incredible proportions. David knew how to be attracted to a woman, how to recognize commitment, and how to be impressed with devotion. But he just did not know how to cherish and follow through on that which had first attracted him. Once he had Abigail, he forgot about her and was on to the next challenge. And in the end, it wreaked havoc upon the entire nation.

Some time ago, I was speaking at the hundredth anniversary celebration of a hospital in the country of Bahrain, founded by the famed missionary Samuel Zwemer. Here at this hospital, over the years, thousands have been treated and shown the love of Jesus Christ. Lives have been brought to birth, and the critically ill have been treated. Pain has been alleviated. And on that occasion we were reminded of the ministry that had taken place at the hospital over one hundred years. But what was most gripping to me during the evening and the walk down memory lane were the words written by Zwemer in tribute to his wife. Put to music by a young Indian woman, they were sung to us beautifully that night. The audience was deeply touched by the words.

Her love was like an island

In life's ocean, vast and wide,

A peaceful, quiet shelter
From the wind and rain and tide.

'Twas bound on the north by hope,
By patience on the west,
By tender counsel on the south
And on the east, by rest.

Above it, like a beacon light,
Shone faith and truth and prayer;
And through the changing scenes of life
I found a haven there.[2]

You see, being able to reach out with love to the masses would have meant little if there had not been a tender heart at home, as well. The song rightly merited the sense of warmth felt by every heart in the room because it spoke of the strength of a love that was kind, a love that gave a haven to a man who served human kind with that same love.

That is how a marriage should be in its depth within and its reach without. It is not at all surprising that the Bible tells us that Rebekah comforted Isaac in the early days of their marriage on the loss of his mother. Kindness is a rare expression, but it is beyond price if the true value of marriage is to be preserved.

Kindness is the touch, the look, the beat of the heart, and the act that seeks to cherish and guard the one to whom you say, "I love you." The commitment of the will and kindness are components that blend in a lovely mix, making a house a home, a haven of precious memories.

4

TO HAVE
AND TO HOLD

Sexual delight without
spiritual truth plunders both.

✣

The first two clues to a godly marriage, parental counsel and the commitment of the will with its flip side of kindness, draw upon our human and cultural wisdom in making the right decision for marriage. Yet with all of our knowledge, we can only know with limited certainty. The Scriptures remind us that as thorough as we might be, we often make our judgments based on outward appearances. So now we enter the stage where God puts His seal on the very character of the person, with particular reference to that which makes the marriage bed sacred.

As Eliezer continues his mission to search for the right person, the emphasis is now on the purity of Rebekah's life. The Scriptures say that she was "a virgin; no man had ever lain with her" (Genesis 24:16). At first sight, the description appears redundant. But the reason for that wording is that the Hebrew word translated here as "virgin" does not necessarily mean biological virginity. It can also be translated "young maiden." So the writer emphasizes the qualification of her youth by the addition that she was also chaste, clearly describing her as a woman who had not taken sexual matters lightly, nor been caught up in some cultural mix of promiscuity. She had treated her body as the temple of the living God.

In giving oneself in marriage, there are few gifts a single, unwedded person can give his or her partner that are more sacred than the gift of purity. I am keenly aware that with the way our cultures have moved globally and the liberties we now take in sexual relations, many appreciate this lesson only after mistakes have already been made. Not only that, there is a growing tendency to see sexual purity as some kind of archaic imposition thrust upon consciences by religion to manipulate people's guilt feelings and, hence, control individual morality through organized religion.

Recently, I read an article entitled "The No Mourning After Pill." A new medication has been developed that chemically affects the brain to relieve posttraumatic stress syndrome—to take away the "mourning" after a heinous act or experience. It is especially helpful in treating soldiers returning from the battle-field, unable to deal with memories of the horrible atrocities they have witnessed. The writer concedes there are legitimate uses of this medication but then presents another fearsome problem that arises. "What use will we put it to," he asks, "if the feeling of guilt haunts a rapist or a murderer? Are we going to eradicate that which nature has intended?"[1]

Fascinating, isn't it? We do not know what to do with feelings of shame and guilt that are legitimate, so we just put them down to "nature." Our philosophical sophistication today has administered ideas that numb the soul and then cavalierly dismisses those who wish to remind us that the feeling of wrong may have been a corrective against the mitigation of the profane. Notions of abstinence or purity are now the subject of academic mockery and are implicitly ridiculed by icons of entertainment. First we dismiss sin with a verbal anesthetic, then we develop drugs to suppress any sense of responsibility. The truth is that even philosophically we ought to be able to see the hypocrisy we are dealing with.

On one occasion a press reporter challenged me by charging that Christians hold to a double standard when they say they are against racism but at the same time are prejudiced against homosexuality. "Is that not somewhat duplicitous?" she chided. I knew she was genuine in her concern, so I said, "Race is a very sacred thing. It is the gift of God to each individual. It is something in which we had no choice or say. We were born with our ethnicity; it is not a culturally assigned quality. Therefore, it should never be violated. In the same way, sex is a gift of God, to be treated with sanctity. We protect sexuality from being violated as much as we protect race from being violated. It is you who have to explain to me why you treat race as sacred and at the same time desacralize sexuality. That is where the duplicity really lies."

There was an ominous silence on her part and then she said, "I have never thought of it that way."

Isn't it amazing that we can go through life holding passionately to our views, yet never pausing to ask ourselves why that view is inviolable? Life and sex are gifts, and marriage shares them to the fullest.

WHY IS IT SO?

Sometimes we wonder what it is about sex that makes it at once one of the most desired and yet mistake-ridden experiences. What is it about the way that we are fashioned that gives us this "good-news-bad-news" combination? It is good news in that sex is pleasurable, bad news in that the parameters seem so stringent. We must go back to the created order to find the answer.

Sex is not something that happened just by accident, nor is it some kind of pragmatic human invention. It is not something that we just came upon and experimented with. Sex was created and planned by God for specific purposes. We have already discussed the first glimpses of Adam's life and made note that God made woman in such a way that she would meet a need for intimacy that was uniquely her privilege and disposition toward man and vice versa. He did not make them identically. If God had merely wanted companionship for Adam, He Himself could have provided it. If He had wanted fraternity, He could have made another man. Instead, He fashioned a woman—equality with a difference and a distinction, psychologically and biologically. These distinctions were undergirded spiritually. This is a point often missed by the average person who argues with tension on matters of gender.

Think for a moment. Are all races equal? Yes. But are there differences? Absolutely. Do those differences make it one's right to dominate the other? No.

Is every member of a family equal in essential value? Yes. Does that mean they are all equal in capacity? No. Does that give one member a right to subordinate the other in terms of worth? No.

Why, then, from the macrocosmic picture of races and the microcosmic picture of families are we not able to lift the lesson for gender relations? The design of God for the first man and woman was to give them unique distinction with purpose and primacy. It was a relationship He designed in such a way that it would take flesh to fulfill—I dare say—in keeping with the spirit.

Even God did not enter into that kind of relationship in that fashion. The reason He made man and woman was that in our physical makeup, physical intimacy bound by the spiritual is something unique to the human relationship. There are indications of what this means in the spiritual realm that must be carried over to the physical. We will get to that.

THE DIFFERENCE
IS MORE THAN IMAGINARY

Recently, I was in a country that is battling the scourge of prostitution on a massive scale. So much money has now become involved that no one dares try to bring it to a halt. In the newspaper articles about all that is going on to perpetuate the financial side of prostitution, I read a most heartbreaking story. Young men, seeing the great profit in prostitution, are having their bodies surgically altered so that they can market themselves to men who desire a female prostitute for the night. The result is now that scores of men who have paid for the services of a prostitute think that they have been with a woman, when all the while they have been with a man who has been surgically altered into a woman for the sheer purpose of making money.

I cannot fathom the extent of this tragedy. In stark terms, it is the sheer folly of the imagination unhinged from reality. It is the physical disfigurement of the body that cheats the pleasure seeker. It is the double-edged sword of each demeaning the other while satisfying the baser instincts at the cost of the other. What is real has been masked, and the result is distortion for one and deception for the other. "What you don't know won't hurt you," they say, but I ask you, Is this not the desecration of what is real? With the incredible strides that science and technology are making, it is more and more difficult to know what is real and what is counterfeit. God reminds us that there is a reality. He has fashioned us for a specific purpose. Gender does make a real difference that is not imagined or engineered.

Having established the basis of the difference between man and woman, we see now that God gives a common ground and purpose that bring the diversities between a man and a woman into unity, a unity that is greater than love. The diversity is not cultural or conditioned by inclination; it is normative. Take a look at this narrative in the Book of Exodus, beginning in chapter 25, to see what we mean here.

Moses went to the top of Mount Sinai in order to meet with God and receive God's instructions for their worship as a people. In that encounter, he was given detailed directions on how to build the tabernacle. One might wonder at such specificity. It was to be so long and no longer, so wide and no wider, so high and no higher. It was to be such and such a color. It was to have a specific number of curtain rods and curtain rings. It was to be a certain shape and have certain dimensions. No one was to touch such and such except so and so. Everything was meticulously presented in a detailed way, and just in case Moses missed it, the design was repeated later in the book with the same precision. We have every right to ask, What is going on here?

We see the answer in some very profound words that we might easily miss at a cursory reading. God says, "Moses, when you have finished building this tabernacle, exactly as I have told you, there I will meet with you. There I will dwell with you" (see Exodus 25:8; 29:44–46). There is a twofold emphasis here—the tabernacle is to be a place of meeting God and a place of communion with Him.

Bring this detail into our modern-day setting. We have local churches where we meet together as believers. We no longer go to Mount Sinai to meet God. Why not? Because the place of the tabernacle and the temple is now replaced by the body—your body and mine—in which God meets with us and God dwells with us, and where we have communion with Him. When we come to the church now, we don't come to the sanctuary; we bring our sanctuaries with us. This individual entity is the locus of appointment between God and me. There He meets. There He dwells. Will the God who went to such pains to physically decorate the tabernacle and the temple not also take great care in physically designing the human body?

During a recent visit to Oxford, England, a local minister took me for a long walk to the chapel at Keble College. It is one of those grand schools with a history as fascinating as its buildings. We walked into the chapel and stood there for just a few moments, saying nothing. Any sound would have seemed invasive. The craftsmanship from centuries earlier brought the realization that for some, this work was that of a lifetime.

We then proceeded to the front, turned to the right and, through a small door, entered a private chapel. There, at the altar, hung one of the most famous paintings in the world, Holman Hunt's *The Light of the World*. Many have seen it, but few study it. The full figure of Jesus, with a lantern in His hand, is standing by a door with no latch on the outside, the path to it overgrown by weeds. It is based on Revelation 3:20: "Here I am! I stand at the door and knock. If anyone hears my voice and opens the door, I will come in and eat with him, and he with me." As Jesus is knocking on the door, the expression on His face leaves you with the uncanny impression that He knows exactly who is inside and longs to have fellowship, if only He would be let in. The lantern symbolizes the conscience; the gently lit face of the Lord radiates a light that is so hard to describe. There is a brilliance that seems to come from within His very being. The conscience is the point of contact; His presence is the indwelling light that reveals what is good and what is evil.

The Lord who made us and knows our struggles comes knocking. He knows the frailties that limit us in the battle and comes to offer a different glimpse, a different strength, and a different path by which to live. That path places a noble value on sexual purity. Is it any wonder that a generation that has become profane of speech and violent in entertainment scoffs and belittles those who wish to treat a person's body as sacred? Sexual promiscuity is condemned in the Ten Commandments for the same reason murder is condemned in the Ten Commandments—it is the marring of the image of God.

THE PURPOSE BLUNTED

If God has reminded us that His desire is to dwell with us and to meet with us in the sanctity of the human body, the violation of that locus destroys its purpose. In an article some years ago, Dr. James Dobson quoted a letter he had received that sums up the ache of a mistake better than I can say it:

> It was as if I physically felt a loss. Throughout our years together, he had taken my self-respect, my self-esteem, my pride, my womanhood, my virginity, my capacity for love, and my future and discarded it as "unwanted." Looking back I didn't realize it then, but when I begged him to come back to me, I lost the last drop of myself. After our final break up, I went on to a Christian college and he went his own way. . . . Two years later, I met and married my husband. My husband is the world to me. He is everything I thought my former boyfriend was or was going to be. He is wonderful to me. We have a lovely home, stable income and beautiful young son who is our joy. However, there is a part of me I cannot share with him, because I gave it to my boyfriend back in high school . . . to me, that is the very private, very painful, very tormenting consequence I cannot change. So the

point is—there is a price. You may or may not pay with preg-
nancy or VD, but you will certainly pay. . . . I know God's for-
giveness, and I continually pray that He will restore the years the
locusts have eaten. . . . Writing this letter has been on my heart
for a long time. Please convey the message to teens and college
students. . . . The consequences you pay most severely and most
personally are paid emotionally.[2]

That is as realistically stated as I have ever read. "The consequences you pay most . . . are paid emotionally." The thing that
spurred you on to act is the very thing you injure—your emotions.
Guarding the act preserves the emotions. Spending in the act
bankrupts the emotions. That is the way God has made us. If you
are someone whom the errors of the past or present still haunt, it
is not my intention to pour oil on the flames of guilt. The realization is painful enough. And that is what I wish to emphasize for
those struggling with this matter while still on the right side of
temptation.

Unfortunately, this seduction has felled kings and robbed them
of kingdoms. It has plundered marriages and broken homes.
It has cost many tears and much heartache. The Scriptures give
us some grim reminders. I borrow first of all from an all-too-
familiar story that is often read so quickly that we miss what is
being said in the fine print of the background.

The story of King David and his tragic alliance with Bathsheba must be read in tandem with a simple incident in David's life years later that speaks volumes of his memory and his recognition of what that relationship had cost him. While the story of his adultery with Bathsheba is given to us in 2 Samuel 11, the incident to which I refer comes to us from 2 Samuel 23. It is one of the last scenes of David's life. In the incident with Bathsheba the nation was at war, while David was at home. In chapter 23 David was again at war and away from home. The Philistines had surrounded the city of Bethlehem and David, separated from his beloved hometown, voiced his longing that he could once more have a drink of water from the well in Bethlehem.

Overhearing him, some of his most fearless men who loved David decided that they would take the risk to bring him water from Bethlehem. In a cloak-and-dagger operation they succeeded in creeping behind the Philistine lines, drawing the water, and getting out again. When they presented David with a container filled with water from the well in Bethlehem, he was surprised and deeply touched. This was when he made a very surprising decision.

As he raised the cup to his lips to drink, he stopped. Suddenly, he realized what an extremely selfish act it was to jeopardize even inadvertently the lives of these brave and loyal men just so that he could get momentary pleasure from that hometown taste. He gradually lowered the cup and then poured the water onto the ground, saying, "'Far be it from me, O LORD, to do this! . . . Is it not the blood of men who went at the risk of their lives?' And David would not drink it" (2 Samuel 23:17).

I bring that little incident before you to ask a question. Why do you think he said that? More to the point, had he said the same thing when he saw Bathsheba while her husband was risking his life to secure David's kingdom, would not all of Old Testament history have been different? In taking Bathsheba, he took what did not belong to him and the result was a trail of death and destruction. That one hour of delight brought the entire nation under the specter of the sword and judgment. One has only to read of the antics of Solomon, son of David and Bathsheba, to notice that the family had caused the entire nation to witness one seduction after another, so that rapacity became commonplace.

Then came that pivotal moment when God denied David's desire and prayer to build a temple for the Lord because of the blood on his hands. He had minimized the sanctity of the human body, and building the temple was not to be his privilege. Reluctantly, God granted Solomon the privilege, but history reminds us of what happened there. Indeed, Solomon built the temple. But soon the temple reflected the people's lives and became a place of spiritual harlotry.

As goes a person's life of sexual honor or dishonor, so goes the possibility of one's worship being true or adulterous. While I am writing these words the well-known basketball star Kobe Bryant finds himself in court, facing the charge of sexual assault. The sad truth about Kobe Bryant's case is that he is known publicly for being a decent, fad-resisting individual. He is one of very few "clean-cut" public figures. Now his fans must wonder if his public persona was a masquerade, hiding an indulgent private life. One newspaper writer had this to say: "People tend to make their deposits into the moral bank accounts in the light of day. But they slink up to the ATM under cover of darkness. How are we supposed to know in the end, whether they're overdrawn or not?"[3]

The answer was given in the article itself. Sooner or later, for most, the moral cost is exacted internally and the external ramifications are only a short distance away.

I cannot reiterate this warning enough. And I must speak especially to young men, and please forgive me for being so blunt. Over the years as I have spoken both on scores of secular university campuses and at Christian institutions, I have found that the differences in actual practice are not very great. That is an alarming fact. Some go to a theological institution thinking they will be in a "temptation-free" zone with halos around their heads. They soon find out that lives are wrecked there, too, in the area of sexual temptation.

A memory of one such college stands out in my mind. I spoke there for five days. I had taken my wife because I had assumed that since my speaking engagements were in the morning and evening, we would be free to have some time together through the day.

I could not have made a more incorrect judgment. As the meetings unfolded and God began to move in the hearts of the students, sign-up sheets for personal appointments were filled every day. I remember two things well. By the week's end I had only one meal with my wife as the rest of the time was spent nursing students through their wounds of regret. The second thing I recall was that of all the students who signed up to talk with me, only one came to talk about something other than sexual failure. That is an indication of what is happening on a typical campus, and the signals are terrifying for the future of the home and the family.

You see, marital vows incorporate a very special commitment—"to have and to hold" cannot apply with the same connotation to any other relationship.

How Do We Protect the Pattern?

The Lord gives us very good insight on how temptation works. In James 1 we see the sequence set forth. Observing how the enemy of our souls sets up the temptation will really clarify how the sequence works.

His first step is to make temptation appear as a natural

desire. It is something unequivocally physical and human. Satan came to the Lord Jesus in the wilderness in the first instance to tempt Him with a natural hunger—the need for bread. As Jesus continued to rebuff him, the devil finally got to the core of temptation. He showed Jesus "the kingdoms of this world" and said, "All this will I give to you, if you will bow down and worship me" (see Matthew 4:1–11).

The key to understanding what is going on here is that "the kingdoms of this world" were ultimately neither his nor his to give. What was he offering, then? It was the enchantment of the eye to go for the shell of existence while losing the essence of one's being. You cannot really have the world and hold on to it. It is all too temporary and the more you try to hold on to it, the more it actually holds you. By contrast, the more you hold on to the true and the good, the more you are free to really live. Where then, does the appeal of temptation lie? It lies in the eyes and in the imagination. One sees without perceiving; the other enjoys without realizing.

The eye is often called the window of the soul. This means, I believe, that not only is it a window through which one may look in, but it is also a window through which one may look out. The best advice I can give a young man is to train the eye. Where the eye is focused, there the imagination finds its raw material. The right focus must be won at immense cost and discipline. Train the eye to see the good, and the imagination will follow suit. It is not at all a surprise that with the invention of television and now the Internet, lives are in serious trouble at younger and younger ages. The imagination is taken captive by handcuffing the eyes.

I remember Billy Graham once being interviewed by English television personality Sir David Frost. At one point Frost asked Dr. Graham if temptation and lust were as much an issue for one in so high a calling, one who walks the straight and narrow so well. Billy Graham looked obviously uncomfortable because it is such a personal subject. He answered it in a very memorable way.

He said that one of his associates was having a campaign in Paris years ago, and on the way back from the meeting, the offerings of the night were hard to ignore. When he got back to his room, he felt such inordinate pressure from the sights he had seen that he was afraid he would make a choice that night that could spell his ruin. It was one of those older hotels that require a large key to lock or unlock the door regardless of which side of the door you are standing. So he locked the door from the inside, walked to the narrow window, and threw the key outside to land in the dirt below. He later told Billy Graham this story and said, "I had to do something that drastic if I was to keep my commitment to God and to my wife." David Frost was obviously quite moved by that story. It was evident that a good man had done the only thing he could think of to do when he knew the situation demanded the absence of choice.

This little illustration has two edges. First is the power of the eye to seduce. Second is the choice to remove the temptation from before the eye. This is the closest metaphorical application I know from the Sermon on the Mount. His eye was offending him, so in effect, he "cut it off." It could no longer see or have access to what was enticing it. The morning would come and the bright light of the sun would expose the deceit of the neon lights from the night before and the clean heart within—I can assure you he felt great in the morning.

This leads to the second step in temptation, the touch. Unfortunately, the one area in which the West has taken a public lead is in the area of touch. Once again, the strength of a relationship is tested when we make it something casual and then profane it. How one touches a member of the opposite sex is a key component of how a situation may develop and where it could lead. This is something we ought not to trifle with.

As a young teenager I learned to dance, and I loved it. It was all in innocent fun, I thought. But it did not take long to realize how easy it is to flirt with danger, for much can be lost when touch and rhythm combine. Around that time I read an author who said something that at the time I thought unrealistic. But with each reading and observation I think he was right. Granted the language is a bit dated, but there is merit to what he said.

The tendency of the modern dance is to take the fine edge off the modesty of both young men and young women. A blacksmith can no more handle the tools of his trade without hardening his hands than a girl can be clasped in the embrace of promiscuous men and still keep her sensitiveness to the questionable and to the unclean. When we consider, therefore, the thousands that are engaging night after night in the modern dances, our wonder is not that so many go wrong, but rather that so many hold their footing upon such slippery places.[4]

He buttresses this point in another context:

Take, for example, our stage folk. They are neither better nor worse to begin with than the average. They are just ordinary human beings. But they play at love-making so much that it loses all its sacredness. Caresses become cheap and common things to be dispensed to almost any passer-by. Such a girl, to use a figure from James Lane Allan, becomes like a bunch of grapes above a common path where everybody that passes takes a grape. He who takes does so without reverence and to his own impoverishment. In the golden coin of real and abiding affection such spendthrifts soon become utter bankrupts.[5]

Where does it all begin? It begins by playing at touch without the real commitment of love. I challenge you to abide by a principle (and only you can seek the mind of God in this) that would be my desire for my children. Be careful, especially in those moments you spend together alone. One principle Margie and I followed in our dating was that we would never be alone together without being accessible to somebody in either a public or a home setting. If we were in her home, we'd be talking in the living room, and when we were in my home, my parents always had access to us. Such precautions aren't absolutely foolproof, but they help reduce the margin of error. The apostle Paul says in Romans 13:14, "Clothe yourselves with the Lord Jesus Christ, and do not think about how to gratify the desires of the sinful nature." In other words, do not put yourself in a place where you can fall.

There remains just one more thing that I would like to say about purity. We are given to think of these qualities as the absence of something—no illicit relationship, no lustful inclination. If we only see purity on those terms, we miss the true nature of what is pure. I want to lift you to see one of the most glorious revelations revealed to any of the apostles, and that was to John the Revelator, in the Book of Revelation, chapter 21.

As John was transported in a vision to heaven, he was utterly surprised by something he did not see. He remarked with utter consternation that there was no temple in heaven. But his consternation turned to joy when he realized that there is no need for a temple in heaven because the Lord Himself is present with His people. There is no need for an intermediary through which to commune with God.

Ultimate purity is a positive state, not a negative state. It is a matter of presence rather than of absence. The immediate presence of God transcends the intermediateness of the temple. In that sense, even the body will one day be shed because God will be all in all. In anticipation of that day, let the temple of the body be pure so that it points beyond itself to the very presence of God in marital commitment. That is why the Lord reminds us that as physical as the sexual act is, the marriage bed remains undefiled because His presence sanctifies the act. That is the privilege of a man and woman coming together in consummating the physicality of love, representing the spiritual bond between the two. For Isaac and Rebekah, that was a covenant worth defending.

5

PREPARING TO LEAVE

Momentous choices are best made when preceded by protracted thought.

As one looks behind the scenes, one cannot help but be intrigued by the discussions between Rebekah's family and Eliezer. Undoubtedly, this is a very Eastern setting. You notice immediately that her brother and mother are doing most of the talking and questioning with Eliezer. This is because in a polygamous situation the father remained in the background and the brother and mother of the girl took the lead. We must also not forget that this was a time (and this is still a culture) in which dreams and visions and portents are taken very seriously. This made for both a sensitivity to supernatural matters and a vulnerability to all kinds of beliefs. That is why Abraham stood out. He was a man of faith who believed in the one true God and trusted Him above all cultural trends and exploits.

Knowing he was backed by Abraham's life and reputation, Eliezer prayed as he journeyed, asking God to give him a sign. When God answered his prayer and gave him the sign, he took the next step and asked to meet her family so that he could explain his mission to them. I would love to have been in on the conversation. He told them of Abraham's charge to him, of his prayer and the fleece he had set before the Lord, and then he brought them up to date on all that had happened in Abraham's life, finally making his proposal for Rebekah to marry Isaac.

This is how the Scriptures tell it in Genesis 24:

"I am Abraham's servant. The LORD has blessed my master abundantly, and he has become wealthy. He has given him sheep and cattle, silver and gold, menservants and maidservants, and camels and donkeys. My master's wife Sarah has borne him a son in her old age, and he has given him everything he owns. And my master made me swear an oath, and said, 'You must not get a wife for my son from the daughters of the Canaanites, in whose land I live, but go to my father's family and to my own clan, and get a wife for my son. . . . The LORD, before whom I have walked, will send his angel with you and make your journey a success. . . .'

"When I came to the spring today, I said, 'O LORD, God of my master Abraham, if you will, please grant success to the journey on which I have come. See, I am standing beside this spring; if a maiden comes out to draw water and I say to her, "Please let me drink a little water from your jar," and if she says to me, "Drink, and I'll draw water for your camels too," let her be the one the LORD has chosen for my master's son.'

"Before I finished praying in my heart, Rebekah came out,

with her jar on her shoulder. She went down to the spring and drew water, and I said to her, 'Please give me a drink.'

"She quickly lowered her jar from her shoulder and said, 'Drink, and I'll water your camels too.' So I drank, and she watered the camels also.

"I asked her, 'Whose daughter are you?'

"She said, 'The daughter of Bethuel son of Nahor, whom Milcah bore to him.'

"Then I put the ring in her nose and the bracelets on her arms, and I bowed down and worshipped the LORD. I praised the LORD, the God of my master Abraham, who had led me on the right road to get the granddaughter of my master's brother for his son. Now if you will show kindness and faithfulness to my master, tell me; and if not, tell me, so I may know which way to turn."

Laban and Bethuel answered, "This is from the LORD; we can say nothing to you one way or the other. Here is Rebekah; take her and go, and let her become the wife of your master's son, as the LORD has directed." (vv. 34–51)

That conversation sealed the understanding and the commitment. There followed an evening of festivities and celebration. Jewelry was exchanged, and the night was spent reflecting on what all this meant. When the morning came, Rebekah's brother and mother asked if she could stay another ten days so that they could properly plan for her departure and give her a ceremonial send-off. After all, they did not know when they would set eyes on her again.

Eliezer did not like the idea of the delay. Sarah had already passed away, and Abraham was ailing. They decided to ask Rebekah what her desires were. She was resolute: If this was the will of the Lord, she was ready to accept it. She said, "I will go" (Genesis 24:58).

On numerous occasions, God spoke directly to young men and women who had walked sensitively before Him and in such special settings that they gladly yielded in submission to His will, even when it was difficult.

Jesus's mother, Mary, is a classic case in point in the New Testament. She was only a teenager when the angel appeared to her and told her that she would give birth to the Messiah. But at that time when responsibilities were given early, the level of maturity was advanced compared to ours. How many teenagers do you know who would have responded with the level of spiritual sophistication and historic awareness that Mary did to the angel's visit—an event on which all of history hangs? There are numerous other women who were entrusted with great spiritual responsibility—Hannah, Deborah, Ruth, Naomi, Elizabeth, and the number goes on. As long as they were certain that it was God's will, they moved forward with courage.

Their youth should not be compared to our youthfulness at the same age. When one notices that King Josiah was only sixteen when he began to seek after God, and only twenty when he led the nation's spiritual revival, we can be certain that the overall process of maturation was significantly different from our day.

But there is something very specific here. The decision of the family to let Rebekah make the final choice is a step that is often forgotten in many Eastern homes today, resulting in many tragedies. Over time, many Eastern marriages have become purely contractual arrangements, discussed and worked out by the parents. It is as if the two young people become just pawns in the brokering of the "deal."

I remember my mother telling me her story of the time that she was supposed to be married. Her parents had arranged everything and the date of the engagement was set. She was simply told whom she was going to marry and that was all there was to it. However, when the day for the engagement came and the house should have been buzzing with activity, nothing seemed to be happening. Everyone was carrying on as if it was a usual day, and not a word was uttered about the engagement ceremony. My mother said she got more and more confused as the day went on. Finally, she asked someone why there had been no engagement ceremony and was told that her fiancé had died a few weeks before in an accident. No one had even bothered to tell her about it. That is how removed she was from a decision of such magnitude. Only heaven knows how much heartache and sadness attend settings where the whole process is so mechanical that the heart and feeling are totally removed from that which God had intended as the closest of all human relationships.

In another instance, the parents of a friend of mine never set eyes on each other until the day they were married. Every time I hear him recount their first meeting on their wedding night, I find it so hard to believe that something like that could actually have happened. When she finally did look upon him that first night, her heart sank with despair. To put it in its kindest way, his looks were quite the opposite of what she had hoped for. Recognizing her anguish, he told her that she owed him nothing and that if she never wanted to share the same room with him he would accept that decision. Every night, he would take his clothing out of the bedroom and sleep elsewhere in the house, never once complaining but making sure she was comfortable and unthreatened. I understand it was months before she decided to give their marriage a chance at survival and share the same room at night. It was the sheer force of his character and courtesy that ultimately won her over.

Stories such as this reveal that no culture has a monopoly on methods, because each of our cultures has found ways to abuse certain privileges and make decisions for all the wrong reasons. The decision to let Rebekah have the last word was very uncharacteristic of her culture and reveals an unusual sensitivity to the importance that she be a willing player in this marriage on her own terms, rather than because of someone else's agenda.

I can say candidly that over the years I have received scores of desperate calls from young people whose parents were forcing them to marry someone of the parents' choice with complete disregard for what their son or daughter may want. Some of these young people, literally on the verge of suicide, asked how they could resist the marriage without being disrespectful of their parents. They are caught in a cultural bind that is the same reason some of them find it so hard to "convert" to the Christian faith when it means having to go against their parents.

In short, just as the young person who is seeking the advice of his or her parents must be respectful of their wisdom, so the parents must never force their decision upon their son or daughter, who must be able to make the choice themselves, readily and willingly. The scriptural injunction here is transculturally stated. When the young couple then bind themselves to each other, they do so by "leaving" the commitment that exists by virtue of their birth in favor of a new commitment that is by virtue of covenant.

That is why the preparation of the heart and will are so critical. This kind of decision cannot be made on the spur of the moment. It must be prayed through and must become part of the character of the individual so that when the decision for marriage is finally made, the prerequisite demands of the soul to be sensitive to the mind of God have already been met. We see only the fruit of such a life. We have not studied the root that made such results possible.

Some time ago I was under some physiotherapy care after back surgery. The therapist had worked with many athletes over the years, and he shared with me what distinguishes a good athlete from a great one. One of the characteristics of greatness is the minimal component of time between the time the mind chooses to act and the muscles fire in response. Michael Jordan in midair, shifting his body weight with lightning speed from one angle to another as he transfers the ball from one hand to the other, is making something almost unimaginable, real. The capacity of Jordan's body to respond to multiple commands from brain to muscle is so instantaneous, almost simultaneous, that it staggers the imagination. Even the slow-motion camera is hard-pressed to pick it up. If the vast majority of us tried the same moves, we would collapse with serious injury—to say nothing of not having the ability. This electric speed was not developed by accident but through discipline and years of preparation. Jordan does what he does because he did what he did. He took his God-given talent and fine-tuned it to make momentary decisions seem just that. The truth is that his mind-body coordination was trained in the silence of empty stands and backyard courts before the public reveled in that skill.

Rebekah may seem impulsive here. Yet the preparation for her decision was already underway, long before this moment. It was instinctive, the legitimate bequest of her habits.

How Does It Begin?

I would like to present three steps that a young person should make in preparation to be able to respond correctly to an opportunity for marriage.

The first is to ask yourself if you truly have the maturity to sacrifice your selfishness for the responsibility that lies ahead. The "reponse-ability" says it all, does it not? Can you respond to what is asked of you in being a spouse and a parent? I was married at age twenty-six. I still remember pondering not whether I loved the girl I was marrying, but whether I had what it took to face the responsibility of living for others and whether I was willing to work hard to provide for her and any future family's needs.

Living with one's parents or with a roommate is actually a very inexpensive way to live, not just economically but emotionally. Someone else pays the emotional bills of running a home. In one way or another you live off the emotional capital of another's expense or minimize your own. It is a little bit like being a student. You really do not face up to the full responsibility of living. You can always hide behind the absolution that this is only a "preparation" stage. When you say, "I do," you enter a whole new world of fiscal, emotional, and manual responsibility.

Think long and hard whether you have reached that mature stage of selflessness for this one you think you love so much. The love you enjoy will be the best thing that ever happened to you, but it will cost you your independence.

Losing your independence means a multiplicity of things. First of all, the work that you do is a means of providing for the family's needs, but the work you do must never become identical to the life that you live. Many homes that have fallen apart would not have done so if it had been understood and acted upon that there is a time to work and a time to leave work. More and more, as our society demands travel and as huge salaries are to be made within corporate structures, in a subtle way, the home has become devalued. Executives, male and female, are made to believe that their real worth is in their corporate success, not in the raising of their families. Every time I see Hollywood icons putting their children on display, it is curious to me that they do it with an inventor's bravado, as if they have discovered some new basis for value: the raising of children. You would think the rest of society that has spent its time in being committed to the family were the ignorant ones and were just awaiting the arrival of this celebrity to point to some new way!

Long ago, the Lord reminded us that the home was a place of sacred trust, and marriage is where it begins. Children spend hours in front of computers and televisions because parents are at work and there is no one to talk to at home.

There was a commercial some time ago that I found very real. A CEO walks into a room crowded with employees sitting around a huge boardroom table. He goes for the jugular right away. "All right!" he says. "Why did you call this meeting? Is the server down again?"

"No," comes the answer.

"Are we outdated on our software?"

"No," comes the answer.

He goes through a barrage of questions on the technical support they constantly rely on. The answer comes repeatedly, "No."

"Then why are we here?" he finally demands in exasperation.

One of the employees says rather sheepishly, with an intonation both asking and answering, "Shirts?"

"Shirts?" he repeats. "What do you mean, 'shirts'?"

"Isn't that what this business is about . . . selling shirts?" the rejoinder comes.

It is easy in the midst of all the trouble spots and support needs to forget the main reason for the existence of the company. Who cannot identify with that? "The computers are down" is a refrain we hear all too often. One would think that the business we are all in is to keep the computers up. Well, let me add to that commercial. We could add to the sales representative's answer by saying, "Home?"

"Home?" he might ask. "What do you mean, 'home'?"

"Do you not have a spouse and children at home to be with, or have shirts become your life?"

The responsibility of marriage and family demands time, and when we cheat on that, we rob ourselves of the investment returns.

PREPARING IN COMMUNITY

The second step in preparing for marriage is to get the best premarital counseling you can. This is a great area of concern that is often neglected by busy clergy, not necessarily by their choice but because of the business of the life of the church. A generation ago, a young person would be in church at least four times a week—for Sunday school and the morning service, the Sunday evening service, the midweek prayer meeting, and youth group. This built a community, and the prospective partners were able to observe each other over a period of time in a setting where their spiritual life was trained and developed.

These days, I know of churches where you sit in front of a screen to watch the service. I am not being critical of this, because the very fact that the congregation is so large and that people are willing to get it secondhand at least concedes that they must be getting something or they wouldn't be there. It is better to be in front of a screen at church than in front of a screen at home, watching heaven knows what. But let us make no mistake about it. This change has turned everything around and results in a new structure. In a very real sense you are no longer a participant but a spectator. You are no longer the one being observed; you are purely the observer. In fact, if the camera were to pan your face, you would be thoroughly embarrassed. You go to see, not to be seen. There is no watchful eye over you, which is part of the accountability training one needs.

Some might say that small groups have taken the place of the fellowship and accountability one used to find in small churches. But small-group dynamics are completely different than a congregational community. In a congregational community you relate across a wide spectrum of ages and callings, and your maturity is tested from every angle. In a small group you only learn to relate to those of similar inclinations and affinities.

Here is an important point. In times of antiquity, the cultural setting provided the impetus for moral development across age and generational barriers. If the culture was strong, moral development was built on a solid foundation. There were balances and counterbalances by generational lines of interaction. As cultures intermixed, values became clouded and the story of a people has been lost by succeeding generations, so that what has actually happened is the loss of a transcending chain of continuity.

Now, as cultures are blended across generations, a whole new ethos is framed, and each generation must reinvent itself without the checks and balances of time and preceding generations. There is no transcending continuity, and the breakdown is drastic. It is not accidental that music has become the focus in many congregations because music has a generational shelf life, where the new music fails to connect with the previous one. Churches have become so "seeker-friendly" that they have become "founder-unfriendly" and have ceased to minister to the older generation, who are gradually being dropped from our society just because they are older. This is the very thing that felled King Rehoboam. His entire political theory was framed by the new generation, who placed no value in the older generation and the wisdom they had acquired (see 1 Kings 12:1–15).

We have replaced the old cloisters in monasteries with new cloisters in huge congregations. Yes, it is important to keep a balance and not be stuck in a particular generation, but we have drawn lines that have made us myopic in our way of viewing things. If church is something you observe rather than an experience of worship, you will be always redefining yourself by whoever is on the platform. That is a dangerous way to define oneself.

A worshiping community should be the fountain from which life flows and the ocean into which your efforts are merged. That is where identity is defined, refined, and consolidated and where continuity remains.

This is why premarital counseling becomes handicapped. When it is done, it is purely on the basis of giving directions, never really providing the opportunity to relate to the Church in light of your growth to marriage. An awful lot can be faked in formal settings of instruction. When our older daughter was married, she received counsel from her pastor, who required the young couple to spend time in a home for the aged and those under special care. He did this because of a very tragic circumstance in his own life.

Shortly after he was married, he was involved in an accident that broke his hands. For months he was unable to use them. He told my daughter and her fiancé that he learned in a hurry what it meant to be loved unconditionally and how menial a task loving somebody can be when you have to take care of his or her every need. His wife suddenly became not just his partner but his nurse and his caregiver in a situation that demanded absolute commitment on her part. One wonders what would happen in most marriages that are put to such a test.

Preparing for Disagreements

There is a third and very important step in preparing for marriage, and that is the commitment to conflict resolution. How do you resolve points of differences, not just in areas of tension but also in areas that become tense by virtue of the newfound relationship? Annoying habits that can be endured from a distance can become nerve-racking when they are under the same roof. The difference with conflict resolution in marriage and conflict resolution in ordinary friendships is that in marriage you marry not just a person but also that person's loves and relationships.

Nobody comes free of other commitments. A young man or woman relates to his or her parents with the benefit of understanding the peculiar norms assumed in their relationship, a benefit that the new spouse does not have. It is not enough to say you will resolve this objectively, because total objectivity is virtually impossible, even as a theoretical framework. With every relationship comes a moral commitment and when all those relationships are blended, it is not merely the blending of two lives; it is the convergence of many lives, the sharpest points of contact being the two who are married.

May I illustrate this in a simple way? When Margie and I were married, we had to decide where we would spend Christmas Day. Fortunately for us, the dilemma was solved very quickly. Both of our parents lived in the same city and for my parents, Christmas Eve was the big day, while for my wife's parents, Christmas Day was the big day. There was no difficulty in spending one day with one family and the other day with the other. I could not believe the number of couples who told us, "You are so lucky to have your parents in the same city so you can resolve the issue." Many couples are not able to resolve this particular problem, either because of distances involved or because the day becomes a tug of war between the two families. The unfortunate thing is that issues like this can bring enormous tension between the young couple and must be talked over so that the relationship is not put in jeopardy over a matter such as this.

But conflict resolution takes on drastic import when matters of personality are at cross-purposes, for one's personality is a distinctive that is not easily correctable. It is for this reason that premarital counseling should focus on personality matters that are significant and will only grow exponentially with time.

Conflict resolution is the key to success in most marriages. Beneath each tension lies one fundamental question: Is the point of tension unresolved because of the issue or because of a disposition? Dispositions are often matters of pride. Demanding a certain solution because of pride sows the seeds for discontent in years to come, yet giving in to the other person's pride is not the solution, either. I once heard a remark attributed to a famous preacher: "Only God knows how to humble us without humiliating us and how to exalt us without flattering us." If God does it that way, must we not seek His strength to do it the same way? Keeping a person humble does not mean to humiliate them. Setting them in a place of respect does not mean to flatter them. Talking it over in the light of the other person's personality is the key to conflict resolution.

Many years ago, I made a key mistake in ministry. Some friends were having a serious problem with a member of their family and asked if I would be willing to talk to him. One receives numerous requests like this and the majority of the times the usual answer should be, "Is that person willing to talk to me?" In this instance, I thought I knew the family well enough and so agreed to meet this friend.

At first, he denied that there was a problem, but unfortunately for him, I had observed the problem firsthand. His face fell when I presented the facts as I had witnessed them. There was a sad moment of pain and embarrassment on his face, and he finally conceded that it was a problem but that he could handle it. I knew that all was not right by his attempt to dismiss the issue with a glib, "It's OK. I'll deal with it."

It was years before I heard from him again. I was told that what had upset him was not that I had talked to him about what was going on but that I had taken a colleague with me into the conversation. My reasons for doing so were first, that my colleague, too, had struggled with the same issue some years before and I hoped that his victorious example would be an encouragement. Second, I have found it wise to have someone with me in such situations so that there is a witness to what I did and did not say. In this instance, it was clearly a mistake because it brought this man a real sense of embarrassment.

I learned a tough lesson here. Doing and saying the right thing are not sufficient. *Doing the right thing in the right way and with the person's comfort in mind is critical.* Thankfully, over the years that rift was healed, and he was magnanimous in winning both that victory and the one that ruptured our friendship for a while.

You see, marriage is a blend—not just of bodies and affections but, ultimately, of two people walking in stride through the hard moments that would divide any other friendship.

It is not at all surprising that Jesus compares His relationship with the Church to that of a bride and groom. Of that relationship with us, Paul says, "Who shall separate us from the love of Christ?" (Romans 8:35). After suggesting several possibilities, Paul answers his own question with an emphatic, "Nothing!" If each partner sees that commitment to be a lifelong one of walking together, in honor preferring one another, marriage becomes beautifully representative of our relationship with Him.

In Matthew 25, Jesus tells the parable of women waiting with their lamps for the bridegroom to come. Some of them have miscalculated the time and run short of oil to keep their lamps burning. When the bridegroom arrives, they are not ready for him.

Before the wedding day, detailed preparations for the ceremony and reception are profuse. How much more critical it is to prepare for a lifetime of togetherness. That requires more preparation than the wedding ceremony. It is the realistic anticipation of blending persons and personalities with differences.

MAKING SURE YOU ARE READY

This true story comes from England. It is the story of a young man named George who was in love with a girl named Mary. Mary and George were engaged to be married, but World War II erupted and George was suddenly called into the army.

Recognizing that this could mean death for him, he decided that he and Mary should wait to be married until after his safe return. So George pled with her, "Mary, please wait for me. After the war is over, I'll come back and we'll get married." Mary agreed.

Many weeks and months went by. George's letters would come and would keep Mary's heart aglow. But suddenly the letters stopped coming. One week, two weeks, three weeks, four weeks, many weeks went by—and there were no more letters. Finally, the family received a communication from the army that George was missing in action and believed to be dead.

Mary's heart was broken. She could not believe that George was really gone. She did not know what to do. As hard as she tried to put her loss behind her, she was not able to get George out of her mind and heart. After several months, she returned home from work one evening and said to her mother, "Mother, I'm really under the weather. I'm just going to go to my room to be alone. Please don't disturb me for anyone." She closed the door behind her and took all of George's letters from her dresser drawer. Lying back on her bed she began to read them again, one by one, as her tears flowed. She picked up George's picture from her dresser, so handsome in his uniform, and held it to her as she continued to read the letters and weep.

For the first time since the news of his loss, she took out her wedding dress that had been bought before George had left. She put it on and stood in front of the mirror looking at herself all bedecked in her gown, holding his picture and the letters, and sobbing her heart out.

Downstairs, there was a knock at the door and her mother went to answer it. She opened the door and grabbed her heart. "George!" she gasped. "What are you doing here?"

George said, "Mother, is Mary home?"

"Yes, but, George, you . . . you . . . you're supposed to be dead!"

"Well . . . ah . . . no . . . I'm all right. Tell me, is Mary married?"

"No, but, George, what happened? We . . . we . . . heard . . . "

George interrupted her gently and said, "Mother, if Mary isn't married, may I see her?" As she stepped aside and motioned toward Mary's room, George headed up the stairway. In England, some of the keyholes are so big you can almost walk through them, and as George looked through the keyhole, he was shocked at what he saw. There stood Mary, just as beautiful as he remembered her to be, in her wedding dress, his picture in one hand, a letter in the other. He opened the door and said gently, "Mary!" She turned toward him in a state of shock and then screamed, "Georgie!" She wrapped her arms around him . . . and I can't continue the story except to tell you that he loosened one arm with difficulty, dipped into his hip pocket, and took out a dog-eared piece of paper. "Mary," he said, "of all the letters you wrote to me, this one was the most precious. I carried it with me through everything. It says this,

'Georgie, dear, I love you. I love you. I love you. And when you come home, I'll be ready.' Darling, I didn't know you'd be this ready!"

Even after all these years of telling that story, it is not possible for me to tell it again without a tear of joy welling up within. What a moment! What a glorious thing it is when a bride and groom meet and they are both ready. The Bible talks of the return of our blessed Lord, when every eye shall see Him. Even the Scripture writers with all of their superlatives find words inadequate to describe this grand moment. The Lord Himself told His disciples that if they were not able to understand earthly things, how would they ever understand heavenly things? We talk of streets of gold, of gates of pearl, of angels, seraphim, and cherubim. I'm not sure we understand the grandness of all of that beauty.

Some years ago I had the privilege of attending the Presidential Prayer Breakfast in Washington for the first time. The thing that stands out most in my memory was the soloist, in the midst of all the world leaders who were present, singing in her soaring soprano voice "The King is coming!" The glorious sound of joyful anticipation filled that grand ballroom of three thousand people and resonated through those walls until President Reagan himself was irresistibly drawn to his feet in applause of what he was hearing—and so was everybody else.

Let us ask God to give us that glorious glimpse of the coming of our Lord. He is the Bridegroom coming for the Bride, and He will come when the Bride is ready for Him. If marriage is as grand as the Bible intended it to be, then it is worth it to wait until you are ready for that right moment . . . for the right one.

6

THE FIRST GLIMPSE,
THE FINAL TEST

*A person stands tallest when
on his or her knees.*

❖

The moment of their first meeting was imminent. Who couldn't be excited? The families must have been curious, and Rebekah most certainly must have been deep in thought. At this point, Eliezer was the only one who had seen both Isaac and Rebekah. There had been no photographs exchanged, no letters, just the tug of God in putting one link into another. As the song says, "This is the moment I've waited for . . ."

I know of no romantic who has not relived the moment of first meeting. I could give you the time and place my wife and I met and the words we first exchanged. I do not know how many times I have been asked the question, "Was it love at first sight?" I think the question is unfortunate because it asks the impossible. How can one truly look back from this vantage point with all that is now known and felt and has been committed to and call what one felt then, love? I can say this, however, that it was truly a tug deep within and, yes, at first sight. The attraction was more than merely looks. There was the impact of a total person. And that attraction grew with time and blossomed into a genuine desire to love and serve.

With each situation, these components may be different, and the specifics ought not to be something upon which one gets trapped into having to explain or explain away. I have also known people who say it was anything but love at first sight. Instead, it was a long friendship that at a certain point turned into devotion and an affection that led to marriage.

For Isaac and Rebekah, the facts were so different. In a very real sense, a nation's destiny was being shaped. Abraham, as we have seen, is probably the most respected figure from that period. He is known as "a man of the tent and altar"—the tent reflecting the temporary nature of life and the altar reflecting the sacredness of life. His faith was proverbial, for at the command of God he had left his home city not knowing his destination. Now that same faith was impelling him at this stage in his life to seek a wife for his son so that together they would raise a family that would stand apart from the pagan practices of the day.

For Rebekah the moment of truth had arrived. As she and Eliezer drew closer to their destination, I have no doubt that her heart must have been beating hard with her fears and anxieties. Only when she had met Isaac could she rest in the complete knowledge that all this had been planned by God.

In the meantime, Isaac, too, had left home and moved closer in the direction to where he would meet up with the arriving party. Only, with no cell phones and no e-mail, it was anybody's guess as to when that day of meeting would come—assuming, of course, that Eliezer had been successful in his mission. For Abraham had told Eliezer that if he did not meet with success, he would accept it as the will of the Lord. There was no guarantee when Eliezer left that he would return with a wife for Isaac.

Gradually, in the distance Rebekah deciphered the figure of a man walking, meditating, and praying. Hebrew scholars are not exactly sure how to translate the word used in this text, but the consensus is that he was in a posture of prayer. The truth is that if someone had been sent on a mission to look for a life partner for me, I strongly suspect I would have been praying at every hour of the day, as well. This is how the Scriptures describe their first meeting:

He [Isaac] went out to the field one evening to meditate, and as he looked up, he saw camels approaching. Rebekah also looked up and saw Isaac. She got down from her camel and asked the servant, "Who is that man in the field coming to meet us?"

"He is my master," the servant answered. So she took her veil and covered herself.

Then the servant told Isaac all he had done. Isaac brought her into the tent of his mother Sarah, and he married Rebekah. So she became his wife and he loved her; and Isaac was comforted after his mother's death. (Genesis 24:63–67)

In an earlier chapter I mentioned that there were a few recurring themes in this story and described the first one, *hesed*, or loving-kindness. The second prominent theme is the constancy of prayer. This entire story is bathed in prayer. Eliezer prayed as he began his mission, as he drew near to his destination, and as he returned home again. Now, as Rebekah gets her first glimpse of Isaac, what is Isaac doing? He is praying.

So often one hears the cynical remark that marriage is not what it is cracked up to be. One might well ask, then, what exactly is it cracked up to be? Is it not the sacred trust of hearts devoted to God, hearts that have experienced His loving-kindness and seek His blessing upon their covenant to each other? If that is what it is, then it is a glorious relationship.

So much is said in these few verses that we can miss the magnitude of what is happening. There is the anticipation within Rebekah's heart. Her life was going to be forever changed. Recall for a moment the blessing with which her parents blessed her as they sent her off: "May you increase to thousands upon thousands; may your offspring possess the gates of their enemies" (Genesis 24:60).

We must not forget that this was not a happy period in the history of the region, and it was a time of serious transition with Abraham approaching his end. So much was going on in various territories, and paganism was at its peak with every tribe having its own deity. It was for this reason that Abraham sent for a wife for Isaac from among his own people: He was concerned that a marriage into a pagan family would so confuse the elements of the faith he had received from God that it would be changed in generations to come. No matter how much we think marriage involves just two people, we find out that is not so. Our times, our surroundings, our culture, economic issues—all come into play. This was a time of tribal warfare and a struggle to keep pure the worship of the true God.

Unfortunately, Abraham had already made a colossal blunder by not trusting God to provide the right heir to his name and faith. From his union with Sarah's maidservant, Ishmael was born. These two brothers, Isaac and Ishmael, were going to change the course of all subsequent history to this very day. Anyone who thinks the violent history of the Middle East is because of recent conflicts just doesn't know history. It all goes back to this very family.

So when Rebekah's family sent her with such a blessing, it was with the hope that she would not be overcome by her enemies and that the promise made to Abraham would remain intact. That is why what happened from here on became so defining for that family and for the world itself.

Very little is said about how Isaac and Rebekah first reacted to each other, but it is evident that their acceptance of one another went as all had hoped it would. We are told that Isaac genuinely loved Rebekah and felt very tenderly toward her. She became a source of great comfort to him, as he was still grieving the loss of his mother.

FIRST IMPRESSIONS AND FIRST THINGS

The first meeting of Isaac and Rebekah revealed much about them. Of all the characteristics that a person needs to be looking for in a mate, I suggest that the individual's prayer life is key to discerning his or her character. I have no doubt that it was a memory upon which Rebekah fell back many times—"The first time I saw you, you were praying."

It is a self-evident truth that a person who truly prays and seeks God's wisdom in life recognizes the sovereignty of God and is committed to seeking God's wisdom in life's important choices. It is important to understand that it is a prayer life that builds character that honors God, not one that brandishes its spirituality or seeks to use prayer as a credential or a badge of honor.

Over the years I have seen so much abuse of even this, one of the most spiritual of all acts, that it can become the worst kind of hypocrisy. I have seen those who all too often think that because they have spent an hour in prayer there is some kind of superiority in them. It would be well in keeping with Satan's deceit of our minds to make even prayer a trap. We must resist that at all cost. Praying is not done in order to wield authority with others or to make an impression. It is done out of a sense of the poverty of one's spirit. A genuine prayer life is one that is constantly broken before God. Such a person's life demonstrates the humility that is born out of brokenness.

This surfaces as a critical pattern needed for a marriage that will last. We have talked so much about our expectation from the partner—kindness, purity, and all that is in keeping with those dispositions. I want to tie this all together with one single principle for you to apply to your own life as I apply it to mine. Become a man or a woman of prayer. Let your devotional life be the beacon that guides you through the tough terrain you will face. Let your heart and mind be kept close to the principal calling of your life, which is to hunger and thirst after God and His righteousness. Make your day one in which God gets your best so that others share in the rewards of your devotion. Let the thoughts and intents of your heart be shaped and guided by time spent in His presence. David talked often about how discouraged or fearful he would become at times. Then he would interject these words, "But then I entered the sanctuary . . ." Being in God's presence affects all other relationships for the better. To have first seen her husband in prayer surely remained a cherished moment for Rebekah.

That classic description of a person walking with God is the same given of Joseph, one of my favorite characters in the Bible. When Joseph was first brought before Pharaoh, he had many qualities that impressed the king. But by far the most impressive quality was the one Pharaoh pointed out to his court. As he listened to Joseph's wisdom and observed his manner, Pharaoh was overwhelmed and said to all of his court assistants, "Can we find anyone like this man, one in whom is the spirit of God?" (Genesis 41:38). This was the reason that Pharaoh trusted him with everything. I think it would be fair to say that any of us would trust any member of our family with a person whose standout characteristic is that the Spirit of God dwells in that individual.

There is an old parable told of a rich man who was going away on a long journey. Before he left he hired a builder and said to him, "I will be gone for many months, and I would like you to build me a house with the specifications I leave with you. I do not want you to substitute anything cheap for the genuine quality that I want. I am willing to pay the price for the best. And when I return, I will pay you for it. But be sure to build it well."

When the rich man was gone, the builder decided to cut corners and to skimp here and there on things that would be hidden from the naked eye and would not be noticed by the owner. The months went by and the builder continued his sly ways that resulted in a house of poor quality while it looked expensive and solid.

Finally, the day came when the rich man returned and inspected the house. After reviewing everything, he said to the builder, "I have a surprise for you. Yes, I will pay for the house, but I want to present this house to you, for you and your family to live in. This is my gift to you."

We may look at some such story and think that is what parables are made of . . . imaginary happenings. But in reality, this is not merely a parable. You may be absolutely sure that as you build your life, so you will dwell. Only for the one in whom the Spirit of God dwells is God the true builder. Only then is a home blessed by God. The single greatest lack of our time, perhaps of all time, is men and women of character, those whose lives are honest and whose transparency is real. I do not know of a stronger witness for Christ than that one be described as a person of true honor.

Some time ago, I was lecturing at a major university, and by the tremendous response both in the numbers of students attending the sessions and in their questions, it was evident to all that God was at work. As the man who had organized the event drove me to the airport, he said something that was quite jolting to me. He said, "My wife brought our neighbor last night. She is a medical doctor and had not been to anything like this before. On their way home, my wife asked her what she thought of it all." He stopped and there was silence in the van for a moment. He continued, "She said, 'That was a very powerful evening. The arguments were very persuasive. I wonder what he is like in his private life.'"

I have to admit it was one of the most sobering things I had ever heard. She was right. Did these lofty truths apply in private as well as in public discourse? The truth is that God calls us to first practice truth in private so that its public expression is merely an outgrowth of what has already taken place in the heart and not a decoration over a hollow life. Developing that strength of character in private is foundational.

To that end, I present three governing disciplines that must translate into life. These sow the seeds of character from which authenticity blooms.

As the Day Dawns

The first is that your personal life must be ordered by prayer as a commitment each day. It should not be seen as a burden but as a privilege to seek the face of God before you face the day. However you order your life, the temptations that will stalk you and the conflicts that will confront or confound you can never be met in your own strength.

Over the years I have had the privilege of meeting many fine people and watching their lives. One such man was Daniel Lam. Daniel was a young man who interpreted for me when I preached in Cambodia in 1974, while I was in my twenties. Cambodia at that time was in dire straits. Under the siege of warring factions, the country was very unsafe. A curfew was strictly enforced. We stayed in some rather uncomfortable places as we moved around the country. When we got to Battambang, about one hundred miles northwest of Phnom Penh and proximate to the famed ancient city of Angkor Wat, he struggled to even find half-decent accommodations. We finally ended up in a building with a stairway built like a maze, with tiny rooms built at every corner of the stairway as it wound its way through that dimly lit structure. Night after night we returned to our little room exhausted from preaching and counseling in sparse churches or in outdoor meetings. Though emotionally strenuous, the week was filled with the thrill of seeing hundreds come to Jesus Christ, including Buddhist priests. One particular night Daniel and I had the privilege of praying late into the night, in a real battle for the soul of a Buddhist priest who had worn the robe for eighteen years. It was truly an emotionally draining night.

Well past our curfew, we walked back in darkness to our upstairs room at the top of the staircase, just under the roof. I figured we were as exhausted as we could ever be. Incredibly to me, at four o'clock in the morning Daniel's alarm went off, just as it did every morning. Quietly, he got up, wound his way in the dark up the stairs to the roof, and in a language that I did not understand but a pathos I could almost touch, he prayed urgently that God would bring Cambodia to a national conversion.

As we were walking to the church later in the morning, I asked him, "Daniel, weren't you too tired to get up this morning?" And he said, "Brother, I was too tired. But if ever I needed to be in prayer on my knees, this was the morning because we'd just been wrestling with the devil for a man's soul."

I have no doubt that those were extenuating circumstances, and I have no doubt that each one of us is "wired" differently, but Daniel's response told me that his confidence really lay in the strength of the Lord. That is what a well-guarded prayer life can reveal about us, that our trust is not in ourselves but in seeking God's strength for what we do. Prayer is not a substitute for action, but prayer undergirds action with the strength that makes the difference.

In one of the most powerful passages of Scripture, John 17, we see the Lord Jesus in prayer. We call this the High Priestly Prayer because Jesus was praying on behalf of His disciples. There are two things in Jesus's prayer that stand out and transfer into the life of a couple wanting to be married. The first is that Jesus prayed to the Father that His disciples "may be one as we are one" (v. 11). If He prayed that for them, how much more must He desire that for a man and his wife who, from the beginning, were intended to be "one"?

But there is something more that He prayed: "That they may have the full measure of my joy within them" (v. 13). His desire was that His disciples would know and experience the fullness of joy that only He could bring within them. Again, I say, if His prayer for His disciples was unity, how much more must that be His prayer for those of us who are united together in His name?

And it is only as we experience that oneness that we experience the full measure of His joy with each other. That should be our prayer right from the beginning. Many pray for the right partner but cease to pray for the right union—that they be one as Jesus and the Father are one and so experience the full measure of His joy in the relationship.

As the Word Instructs

The second part of shaping character is to study God's Word with a disciplined regularity. The Psalmist reminds us in Psalm 119:105 that God's Word is a lamp to our feet and a light for our path. He also says in the same chapter, "To all perfection I see a limit; but your commands are boundless" (v. 96).

That is an incredible statement. We think of commands as restrictive, binding, and limiting. The Psalmist came to see God's commands as a boundless terrain of pure delight. That is what the Word is intended to be. Early in my life, I picked up a Bible study guide written by Robert Murray McCheyne, the famed preacher from Dundee, Scotland. McCheyne went into the ministry when his brother suddenly died. He spent a disciplined life in the Word and in prayer, and before his death at less than thirty years of age, he was used by God to usher in one of the greatest revivals ever known in Scotland. McCheyne taught his parishioners to read through the Scriptures every year. That meant reading two chapters from the Old Testament and two chapters from the New Testament every day. Included in that was a repeat of the Psalms and Proverbs each year.

The advantage of a planned study is experiencing the marvelous way in which God in His sovereignty brings certain passages before you just when you need them most. The second thing about a systematic study is that if you ever miss a day of Scripture reading, you know exactly where to pick it up again. One of the tragic things about growing up in a Christian home is that often we learn so much subliminally that we fail to make a study of the Scriptures ourselves. Learning, studying, and memorizing make an inscription in the very soul. You never know when you will need a word from the Lord in a particular situation, and if you are in the Word regularly, God has a context within which to reach you.

But I caution you again. I have known people who study the Scriptures, quote the Scriptures, and have every page marked and underlined, but their single purpose seems to be to use the Scriptures to attack others or to prove anything they want to prove while their lives show anything but the grace of God. The single greatest purpose of the Scriptures is to make you "wise unto salvation" (2 Timothy 3:15 KJV), meaning that it leads you to the Savior and then becomes a source of instruction to help you grow in character and wisdom. It is to equip you and make you presentable to God.

When we lived in England for a short while, we experienced one of the most violent windstorms that had ever hit England. More than 750 thousand trees were felled in one night. Some days later we were walking in the parks past huge trees that had been completely uprooted by the wind. My wife noticed how shallow the root systems were on some of those massive trees. When we mentioned this to someone, they pointed out that in England the water table is so close to the surface that the roots of the trees do not have to penetrate deep for nourishment. As a result, the trunk grows in disproportion to the roots. When a severe storm hits, these gigantic trees are uprooted because there is nothing to anchor them.

What an illustration that is of a life without prayer. You can be sure that in every marriage the storms will hit. It is in your deep immersion into the Word that your roots will be able to hold the home together. The Word should be the foundation of your home.

It is not at all surprising that as the Church has become illiterate in the Scriptures, it has resembled the world more in its behavior, uprooted by every new fanciful philosophy and fad.

As the Worship Binds

This leads me to the third step, which is active involvement in a local church, especially when the family is young and needs to grow in faith and knowledge. Being active in a local church teaches you together and builds you up with shared experiences in spiritual things. Church is also a place where you learn to relate to others and prove that in your other relationships you can keep this one relationship singularly pure. It is the place where you learn to give, to support the work of the Lord, and to gain a vision for the world in reaching out with the gospel. It is the place where you will build your memories and find a support group to stand with you. The Church is as much instituted as your marriage, and in spite of all of its failings, it is the place where you learn to worship as part of a larger community. It is the place where you sing and study God's Word. It is the place where you meet and talk with fellow believers. It is the place where you learn to bear one another's burdens and so fulfill the law of Christ (see Galatians 6:2). It is a place that you need, and it is a place that needs you.

We can talk all we want about dating and all we want about romance, but as I bring this challenge, I ask you: Are you willing to be a man and a woman of prayer so that as you are deeply devoted to God, He will reveal to you the partner for your life and make you to be the person God wants you to be?

For Isaac and Rebekah, the first meeting was very auspicious. From that meeting a home and a nation were built. It meant that she gave herself totally to him, even as he gave himself totally to her.

Several years ago, I read the following article on marriage in *Reader's Digest:*

Marriage means handing over your whole self—your body, your soul, your happiness, your future—to the keeping of one whom you love, but who is, and remains, greatly a stranger. This tremendous act of faith is something that can unlock in each lover powers of compassion, endurance, generosity, joy, passion, fidelity and hope that no one guessed were there. That is why the confidence of young lovers is not arrogant or foolish but an expression of a basic fact about human nature: the fact that the greatest of human gifts are set to work only when people are prepared to risk everything.[1]

But such a risk is taken only after you have risked everything for God.

7

FACING REALITY
AND EACH OTHER

*Life has its luggage, but God has promised
to carry it for you.*

✜

E ven when all the right efforts have been made and everything
has fallen into place before marriage, why do marriages so often
go wrong? This may be the most difficult question to answer as
far as marriage is concerned. I have known couples who have
shared and treasured the best of experiences and years, and yet
almost imperceptibly comes a weakening from within. Gradually
their lives fall apart. There seems to be no romance left, the
house becomes merely a dwelling place, and there is deep inside
a terrifying feeling that something is not right. This is not the
feeling of betrayal or infidelity or of wanting out. It is just a
sense that the cup has been drunk to the full and there is nothing left. There is a romantic fatigue—all the elements are in
place, but there is no fire.

Sometimes there have been drastic indications of trouble,
although at other times there are not. In a society where both
partners work, there is bound to be added strain on the relationship because their lives are locked into different worlds for the

better part of each day. It used to be that when one partner was out of the home working, the other partner carried the primary responsibility of keeping the marriage intact. But with the way economic growth and possibilities have risen the world over, the pressure to secure a strong financial base has grown exponentially, which has meant that both partners work outside the home.

But the pressure is more than just financial. We have a built-in desire to use our minds and capacities, and building a home does not present the same dynamic attraction as a career. Unfortunately for us, rather than keeping the marriage in its place of priority and finding solutions to the problems, we argue over who gets the long end and who gets the short end of the cultural stick.

A man once came to me and said he was struggling with an issue. He was being asked to play, in his words, "Mr. Mom," because his wife wanted to work full time. She felt it was important for one of them to stay at home with the children, and she said it should be him. "I feel very confused about my role and sit at home terribly depressed. I am the homemaker, dad, and mom, all in one."

I knew this would be a hard thing to sort out in a one-time conversation. But as it happened, a couple of days later his wife came to me and asked rather sharply if I thought she was wrong in the position she had taken. By her tone and expression I was even more certain that the problem was far deeper than just this.

I told her that what I thought of her position was really very secondary to the situation. "You had better be sure you are doing the right thing," I said, "because the home is headed for trouble with the emotional cost of the position you are holding. At the very least try to find some middle ground, and that is all I have to say. You need professional counsel for this."

The issue here, really, was not who should stay home and who should go to work. Neither wanted to stay home, but one demanded that the other should comply. The result was a ticking time bomb.

That is just one illustration. There are scores more of a different sort. The issues are far too complex to try to sort out here, but I would like to take a stab at what can go wrong and how to keep it from happening.

"I DESERVE BETTER"

First and foremost, do not even flirt with the idea that there may have been somebody better out there or someone else with whom you may connect better. Infidelities are not always physical. Emotional vagaries of the mind can be equally dangerous to the health of one's marriage. Mind games can bring bigger losses than imagined and should be stifled early. Receiving the partner as a gift from God, "warts and all," is a commitment with which one begins. The hard thing about this is that both of you need to deeply believe this. One person alone on the path of unconditional love can find it terribly exhausting.

A sincere soul-searching is the most important step when trouble looms large. Affairs often begin because one person finds someone else he or she relates to better and with whom he or she experiences more intimacy or warmth, without all the burdens of carrying a family. It may just be that many marriages break up after years of raising a family because the concerns that have been shared after half a lifetime of bearing one another's burdens are too big to carry any longer. But this is where we have to step back and realize what love and marriage are all about. Marriage brings together not just a man and his wife but their children and their struggles. To suddenly drop the partner who has carried that load with you along life's journey for all these years for someone with no strings or worries attached is cruel. Marriage is not a commercial enterprise in which you replace a car you have tired of with another one. The truth is that the new car will lose its appeal, too, to say nothing about yourself. Someone has said that a man owes his success to his first wife and he owes his second wife to his success.

From its very inception, kill the thought that there is somebody better out there, with arms wide open, just waiting to bring you perfect happiness. Freedom from joint responsibilities and concerns is always idealized in the short term but is never realized. The greater the degree of immersion in another's life, the greater is the "pain" of living. That is just the way it is. The greater the involvement in another's life, the greater is the demand for sacrifice. We are not here to be coddled and made to feel better. There is no perfect person out there, and "better" can be a very misleading term.

Having said all of that, there are some evidences in Isaac and Rebekah's marriage that show how even two good people ended up making serious blunders along the way. Their love for each other was never in question, but there were numerous problems in their relationships with others that brought tension between them.

The first time we see chinks in Isaac's armor, Isaac and Rebekah were living in Philistine territory during a famine in the land. The Philistines watched him closely and, out of fear that his hosts would kill him because Rebekah was so attractive, he pulled a dangerous stunt.

This is how the Scriptures tell that incident, in Genesis 26:

> When the men of that place asked him about his wife, he said, "She is my sister," because he was afraid to say, "She is my wife." He thought, "The men of this place might kill me on account of Rebekah, because she is beautiful."
>
> When Isaac had been there a long time, Abimelech king of the Philistines looked down from a window and saw Isaac caressing his wife Rebekah. So Abimelech summoned Isaac and said, "She is really your wife! Why did you say, 'She is my sister'?"

Isaac answered him, "Because I thought I might lose my life on account of her."

Then Abimelech said, "What is this you have done to us? One of the men might well have slept with your wife, and you would have brought guilt upon us."

So Abimelech gave orders to all the people: "Anyone who molests this man or his wife shall surely be put to death." (vv. 7–11)

The Bible never hides the scars of its heroes. You wonder why Isaac lied about his wife. We know that his father, Abraham, did the same thing in the same town when he was in a similar situation. Did this pragmatism carry over by upbringing, or was he just part and parcel of the culture of that day, with a stock of convenient lies to help him get by? Or was it just sheer lack of faith that God would help see them through? Strangely enough, the Scriptures tell us nothing of how Rebekah felt.

What we do learn is that anytime you put your spouse at risk in order to protect yourself, you demean her worth and exalt your own. We may not find ourselves in as dire a circumstance as Isaac was as he feared for his life. But often we do try to make impressions upon people at the cost of our spouse. I have been in cultures where one spouse is made to look weak and silly in an attempt to be funny. This kind of trivial or serious belittling cuts away at the heart. The very word *sarcasm* literally means "cuts the flesh."

In diminishing the other we devalue ourselves. Respect and dignity are an intrinsic part of valued relationships. I have no doubt we have all made those mistakes, but rather than excusing them, we should correct them.

It is ironic that in the cases of Abraham and of Isaac, the pagan rulers rebuked them for what they had done and recognized how serious the consequences could have been by putting the women at risk. Often in the much lesser circumstances that we find ourselves, it is not uncommon that someone of a different faith will notice the disrespect or censure with which we treat our spouse. This is not good for the marriage, for the children, or for one's witness for Jesus Christ. Familiarity ought not to breed indifference to one's self-worth.

Heartbreak for the Parents

As one follows the story, we see a moment of great sorrow that befell this household. In Genesis 26:34–35 we read, "When Esau was forty years old, he married Judith daughter of Beeri the Hittite, and also Basemath daughter of Elon the Hittite. They were a source of grief to Isaac and Rebekah."

Isaac and Rebekah's marriage had now reached the stage where it was time for their children to marry, and unlike his parents, the older one is going to do it without their blessing. Esau did not concern himself with his parents' counsel and married not just one but two women of a completely different faith. This was utterly crushing to Isaac and Rebekah. Only after some years when a serious break had come between their children, Esau and Jacob, do we read that Esau realized for the first time how much he had grieved his parents by marrying somebody outside his faith (see Genesis 28:8).

That heaviness wore down Isaac and Rebekah because their entire commitment to each other was built upon the hope of bringing children into the world who would carry Abraham's blessing, generation after generation. Now, the oldest had squandered that birthright.

Watching your child go astray is one of the greatest burdens anyone can ever carry. I have seen it and the heart never beats the same under such a heavy burden. This happens in godly homes as well as in homes where God is not honored. There is no easy answer as to why it happens, and one can never be sure of the end result until the end comes. For some, the child's departure from their commitment to the Lord is short. For others, it means a long road of disobedience. For yet others, they turn their back upon faith and family and never return. There is nothing—not even death—as painful to a godly parent as a child in rebellion against God.

Many years ago, I read a book called *Father and Son* by Edmund Gosse. Edmund's father was a well-educated marine biologist who, in the face of the writings of Charles Darwin that

were newly popular at that time, nevertheless clung to his belief in
God and remained a committed Christian. But Edmund himself,
equally if not more accomplished, moved in circles that gradually
gave him the courage to tell his father he had lost his faith.
Edmund's credentials included his prestigious position as assistant librarian at the British Museum and then librarian at the
House of Lords. When he informed his father that he had turned
away from his faith in Jesus Christ and could intellectually no
longer believe, his completely brokenhearted father wrote this letter that Edmund quotes in the last page of his book after their fellowship with each other was broken as well:

> Son . . . when you came to us in the summer, the heavy blow
> fell upon me: and I discovered how very far you had departed
> from God. It was not that you had yielded to the strong tide of
> youthful blood, and had fallen victim to fleshly lusts; in that
> case however sad, your enlightened conscience would have
> spoken loudly, and you would have found your way back to the
> blood which cleanseth us from all sin, to humble confession
> and to self-abasement, to forgiveness and to re-communion
> with God. It was not this; it was that horrid insidious in-
> fidelity, which had already worked in your mind and heart
> with terrible energy . . . nothing seemed left to which I could
> appeal. We had, I found, no common ground. You were thus
> sailing down the rapid tide of time towards eternity, without a

single authoritative guide (having cast your chart overboard),
except what you might forge upon your own anvil.

This dreadful conduct of yours I had intended, after much
prayer, to pass by in entire silence; but your apparently sincere
inquiries after the cause of my sorrow have led me to go to the
root of the matter . . . it is with pain, not in anger that I send it;
hoping that you may be induced to review the whole course, of
which this is only a stage, before God. If this grace were granted
to you, oh! how joyfully should I bury all the past, and again have
sweet and tender fellowship with my beloved Son, as of old.[1]

Every time I read those words I cannot fight back the tears. I can
feel the ache of the father. Any parent who has experienced this
break is crushed under the weight of sorrow. The world looks different when you feel you have lost your child. In this instance, it
was not that the son had become a debauched individual. If that
had been the case the father would still have hope, because those
who are engaged in an indulgent lifestyle know that there is an
emptiness within and can turn when that realization is admitted.
No, this was far worse. This was a rebellion of the mind. Edmund
had reasoned his way out of God, and the father said there was no
common ground of authority left between them. You see, when
there is a measuring stick one can show truth from falsehood.
When there is a determined effort to disbelieve and reason is called
to aid in that disbelief, even when it is shown to be spurious, there

results a huge chasm. Their fellowship was ruptured and the senior Gosse lived with a shattered heart.

Work hard at keeping in tune with the way your children think. Your efforts may not always bring the desired result, but we must do our part. Keep close contact with them. Teach them with regularity, both by word and by deed. Love them and let them know you care for them because of who they are and not for anything else. Answer their questions with candor and thoughtfulness. Do not ignore their struggles. Deal with their difficulties, and spare them a cynical attitude. Stay tuned in to their struggles. Most of us learn the hard way that our children were in a very different world in their own thoughts than we realized.

Fathers especially need to have an impact on sons, because there are fewer and fewer examples of godly men for young men to follow. Dr. James Dobson has said that mothers raise boys; fathers raise men. I have met many a young man whose father has been negligent and who longs for a dad's hug or embrace. This is not because daughters are any less needy, but they have an example in their mother's presence. Boys are left in an island of confusion with no one to model for them the way out. There is little doubt that men have led the way in the dereliction of duty to the family.

At a time when their children falter, it is imperative for friends to encourage and strengthen the family. Unfortunately at this their loneliest time many pass judgment rather than offer comfort. Love and prayer are two of the most important components as parents wait for their beloved son or daughter to return to faith. At the sunset of life, this must be left completely to God who knows what is best.

THE TENDER NERVE OF CULTURE

For Esau not to have known how grievous this was to his parents reveals much about his own spiritual indifference. Marrying outside of both his faith and his culture was, at best, a huge burden to put on a marriage. Someone has said, "Religion is the essence of culture and culture the dress of religion." I believe that is a significant definition of culture as it relates to religion, but it is far from exhaustive in defining what culture really means. This is a highly sensitive topic in our times and is easily misunderstood.

Over the years I have received numerous calls on this subject, probably because ours is a cross-cultural marriage. Culture is critical in marriage because in a real sense, culture is the behavioral expression of one's values, appreciations, tastes, and relational style in both simple and serious matters of life. Add to this the dimensions of language and cultural memory, and you have worlds within worlds. In effect, culture provides the how and why of an individual's behavior. That is why culture is a factor both within an ethnic group and outside an ethnic group. Some cultures I have lived among would unblushingly admit that they would not even think of marrying someone from within their own culture whose subculture is radically different from theirs.

During the war in Vietnam, I attended the wedding in Saigon of a lovely young Vietnamese woman and an American serviceman. They sat through the whole evening saying absolutely nothing to each other because they did not speak the same language, and the bulk of the guests spent much of the time talking about their silence. This kind of divide can be crossed for some, but let us be sure that language was just the tip of the iceberg. There was a difference in the very souls of their cultural background, their frames of reference for their past, present, and future.

Of greater challenge than language are the values and interpersonal treatment of individuals. I was in one culture where night after night after I had finished speaking, a different woman each time would come and ask if she could talk in a setting where she could not be overheard. Their stories were all the same. They lived in a culture where it was customary for their husbands to stop at a bar or some other such setting on their way home from the office to have emotional and physical needs met by other women before they headed home for dinner and to the family. For these women, that acceptance of their husbands' behavior by their culture was nothing more than patriarchal domination that gave the blessing of society upon men and their adulteries. The soft tones in which these women shared their grief veiled a scream of hurt from within.

On numerous occasions somebody has said to me, "I will never marry within my own culture, because I know the abuse I will have to put up with to accommodate the prejudices we hold here." I could write a whole book on the pain with which many live in their marriages. For some it has even ended in suicide.

As you can see, culture is not just an interethnic thing; it is intraethnic as well. For Isaac and Rebekah their faith was critical, but let us be certain their values were in jeopardy when their son married someone of a different cultural persuasion. Culture is a real thing. It transcends ethnicity as it encompasses the habits of the heart and mind with a tenacious grip. Marriage does not always release that grip, and it can choke the romance out of two eager young people who thought they could make it work. Cultural affinity in determining a marriage partner is never to be minimized.

GIVING GOD A HAND

We come now to the most difficult area of Isaac and Rebekah's struggle at home. When Rebekah was pregnant, God revealed to her the destiny of her sons:

Two nations are in your womb,

and two peoples from within you will be separated;

one people will be stronger than the other,

and the older will serve the younger. (Genesis 25:23)

The birth of these twins was no ordinary event. They would shape history, and God was going to reverse the normal trend. The birthright to inherit the father's succession was the prerogative of the older one. But in this instance, God was going to give the birthright to the younger son. Jacob, not Esau, would take the mantle of Abraham.

There were early signs of Esau's propensity toward making the wrong choices. On one occasion, when he was tired, he and his scheming brother got into a discussion over some food. Jacob offered to give Esau his food if Esau would trade away his birthright. An incredible demand and an even more incredible willingness to throw it all away for a meal! Esau was clearly a pragmatist, willing to trade away his destiny for a moment's satisfaction.

Several years later when Isaac was old and his eyes were weak so that he could no longer see, he called for Esau so that he might impart the birthright blessing on him. He asked Esau to prepare him a meal of fresh game, and with that meal he would transfer the trust to him. It was at this point that the family, with the best of intentions, engineered and deceived each other, each one thinking they were doing God's service. Rebekah overheard the conversation between Isaac and Esau and rushed to Jacob to suggest that he pose as Esau and receive the blessing from Isaac. The two contrasting blessings that Isaac gave his sons tell us what lay ahead for these two men.

To Jacob, thinking he was Esau, Isaac said:

> May God give you of heaven's dew
>   and of earth's richness. . . .
> May nations serve you
>   and peoples bow down to you. . . .
> May those who curse you be cursed
>   and those who bless you be blessed. (Genesis 27:28–29)

When Esau returned and realized what had happened, the Bible says that he "wept aloud" and begged his father for any blessing he could receive. But alas, he had sown the seeds of his own discontent, and now no manufactured blessing would change the course that was his lot—to lead a "restless" life (see Genesis 27:39–40). To protect Jacob from any vengeful act Esau might plan in retaliation, Rebekah sent him to her brother's home, never to see Jacob again. This entire episode is steeped in tragedy and deceit.

It is interesting to me that nowhere are we told of Isaac and Rebekah sitting down and discussing this situation or seeking the best solution to their problem without bringing such deep division in their family. One has a great sympathy for Rebekah in this because she knew that the promise was to be inherited by Jacob. But by her maneuvering she encouraged the scheming heart of Jacob, annoyed the rebellious heart of Esau, and set in motion a countermove against Isaac. This is a classic case of how spiritual convictions with an overaggressive will can actually reveal a lack of faith rather than the very faith they seem to demonstrate. Rebekah thought she would accelerate the march of history by this act when, in fact, she may have influenced some of the conflicts that would come.

Serving God and playing God are two different things. In raising a young family, we often come across the need to instruct and prepare our children, but we must be careful that we do not engineer their minds into God's plan for them. I have no doubt that this was not an easy situation for Rebekah, but did she really think that, outside of her duplicity, God had no way to bring the blessing to Jacob that He wanted?

We do this in lesser ways. We tend to conduct devotions with our children or other settings of organized instruction with such rigor that we forget that the best teaching sometimes comes as incidental to the setting, not in some formal force-fed structure. We set up spirituality and then are surprised that the end result is set-up spirituality.

Isaac was an old man when he gave the blessing. Decades had gone by in which he could have considered the best way to transfer the blessing. By waiting to the last minute, he set a divided course for the family.

The Joy of Accomplishment

All said and done, God honored His promise to Isaac and Rebekah. We want to turn our attention now to that pivotal moment in Jacob's life when the years had gone by and he was on his way back home to meet Esau. Isaac and Rebekah had died, and all Jacob's fears of revenge at the hand of Esau were before him. Fearful of what the next day would bring between him and Esau, Jacob spent the night in prayer, crying out to God to bless him. The all-seeing God asked Jacob for his name. Jacob knew he had been cornered. This time he could not lie, as he had lied to his father years before. He admitted who he was, and God said that because of the change in Jacob's heart, evidenced by his admission of who he really was, God would change his name to Israel and would make a great nation out of him (see also Genesis 35:10 and 46: 3–4). Out of the spoils of scheming and manipulation, God was still able to rescue and bring greatness.

All of this is a reassuring reminder that in spite of our mistakes and failures, our heavenly Father is still able to bring something lasting and beautiful from our lives. The description of the tender reunion between Jacob and Esau in Genesis 33 is very touching: "Esau ran to meet Jacob and embraced him; he threw his arms around his neck and kissed him. And they wept" (v. 4). Unfortunately, Rebekah was not there to see God restore what had been lost.

Jacob proceeded to introduce his family and his entire entourage to Esau. Then he paid Esau the ultimate compliment: "To see your face is like seeing the face of God" (v. 10). What a moving tribute.

The key to all relationships and to reconciliation is for each party to be willing to see the face of God in the face of the other. We may walk with a limp, but we will be headed in the right direction. Age or sickness may weaken us, but the sight of a divine feature even meagerly reflected will remain enchanting. Struggles will come, but we steady each other with His arm. Sometimes there may be silence, but we continue to listen closely for His lips to speak. Sometimes we may see darkly, but His eyes continue to give direction.

Marriage brings face to face two people committed to God whose face is distinctively revealed in each as they see each other in the light of God, shining on each countenance. God brought them close to each other because each was the other's answer from God, to rescue them from being alone.

I am not a fisherman, but the other day I read some simple rules for fishing. One was this: Be sure your face is toward the light! The skillful fisherman will always see that the sun shines upon his face and that his shadow falls behind him. He who turns his back to the sun and lets his shadow darken the stream has said good-bye to all the trout.

That is a helpful metaphor for enjoying the delights of marriage. Each day, take a good look at that face before you and see, in the light of God's grace, the face of God reflected in that precious face. Know that while each distinct feature is unique there is a common blueprint for both of you. See the beauty or frailty, as the case may be, as the characteristic given to the individual and the trust given to you. The embrace, then, is an embrace of pure love and trust. Don't turn your back to the other's plea. As you look at each other face to face and see the face of God, you move the home and history in the right direction. May that be our joy and hope.

I began this book with the vivid memory of attending my first Christian wedding. The impact was real. One of the clearest challenges to me was from the opening hymn that was sung. I read the words several times.

> The voice that breathed o'er Eden,
> That earliest wedding-day
> The primal marriage blessing,
> It hath not passed away.
>
> Be present, heavenly Father,
> To give away this bride,

As Eve thou gav'st to Adam
Out of his own pierced side.

Be present, gracious Savior,
To join their loving hands,
As Thou didst bind two natures
In Thine eternal bands.

Be present, Holy Spirit,
To bless them as they kneel,
As Thou for Christ the bridegroom
The heavenly spouse dost seal.

O spread Thy pure wings o'er them!
Let no ill power find place,
When onward through life's journey
The hallowed path they trace,

To cast their crowns before Thee,
In perfect sacrifice,
Till to the home of gladness
With Christ's own bride they rise.[2]

Read these words carefully. It will take you back to Eden. It will take you to the focus of the relationship within the Godhead. It will remind you of the One who gives you away, the One who blesses with the miracle of bringing you and your spouse together as you kneel before Him, the One who indwells you to help you carry out your commitment, the One who protects you through the storms that will come. Finally, lift your gaze beyond yourself to the One who comes as the ultimate Groom, having prepared a home for you.

Marriages that are Christ-centered are beautiful to behold and wonderful to enjoy. Romance as God intended it can last a lifetime.

NOTES

INTRODUCTION

1. Dr. David Popenoe and Dr. Barbara Dafoe Whitehead, "Sex without Strings, Relationship without Rings" from *The State of Our Unions, 2001,* paper published by The National Marriage Project, http://marriage.rutgers.edu/publications/pubsexwostrings.htm.

CHAPTER 1

1. Mortimer Adler, *The Synopticon: An Index to the Great Ideas,* vol. 1 (Chicago: Britannica, 1952), 543.

2. Peter Kreeft, *For Heaven's Sake* (Nashville: Thomas Nelson, 1986), 18.

CHAPTER 2

1. William Doherty, *Take Back Your Marriage* (New York: The Guilford Press, 2001), 11.

2. G. K. Chesterton, "A Defence of Rash Vows" in *The Defendant* (New York: Dodd, Mead & Company, 1904), 23.

3. Quoted by William Doherty in *Take Back Your Marriage*, 7.

CHAPTER 3

1. Daniel Block, *Judges, Ruth,* vol. 6, *The New American Commentary* (Nashville: Broadman & Holman, 1999), 605–606.

2. Words of stanzas one and two by Samuel Zwemer. Stanza three added by Dr. Paul Armerding, who is present director of American Mission Hospital. Found at http://www.amh.org.bh/pages/cenceleb.htm csong.

CHAPTER 4

1. Erik Baard, "The No Mourning After Pill," *New Straits Times* (19 August 2003), P1.

2. Quoted in *Family News from Dr. James Dobson*, August 1992, 5.

3. Steve Aschburner, "Is Kobe's 'Moral Bank Account' Overdrawn?" *AOL Exclusive,* 23 July 2003, at http://www.aol.com.

4. Clovis G. Chappell, *Home Folks* (Grand Rapids: Baker, 1974), 94.

5. Ibid., 26.

CHAPTER 6

1. "The New Meaning of Marriage," condensed from *Réalitiés* by Rosemary Haughton for *Reader's Digest* (January 1971), 81.

CHAPTER 7

1. Edmund Gosse, *Father and Son* (Middlesex, England: Penguin, 1983), 250–51.

2. "The Voice That Breathed O'er Eden." Words by John Keble (1792–1866).